CHICA,
WHY NOT?

Hay House Titles of Related Interest

YOU CAN HEAL YOUR LIFE, the movie,
starring Louise Hay & Friends
(available as an online streaming video)
www.hayhouse.com/louise-movie

THE SHIFT, the movie,
starring Dr. Wayne W. Dyer
(available as an online streaming video)
www.hayhouse.com/the-shift-movie

***

The Law of Attraction: The Basics of the Teachings of Abraham
by Esther and Jerry Hicks

Mirror Work: 21 Days to Heal Your Life by Louise Hay

The Power of Intention: Learning to Co-create Your World Your Way
by Dr. Wayne W. Dyer

Witchery: Embrace the Witch Within by Juliet Diaz

All of the above are available at your local bookstore,
or may be ordered by visiting:

Hay House USA: www.hayhouse.com®
Hay House Australia: www.hayhouse.com.au
Hay House UK: www.hayhouse.co.uk
Hay House India: www.hayhouse.co.in

CHICA, WHY NOT?

How to Live with Intention and Manifest a Life That Loves You Back

SANDRA HINOJOSA LUDWIG

HAY HOUSE, INC.
Carlsbad, California • New York City
London • Sydney • New Delhi

Published in the United States by: Hay House, Inc.: www.hayhouse.com®
Published in Australia by: Hay House Australia Pty. Ltd.: www.hayhouse.com.au
Published in the United Kingdom by: Hay House UK, Ltd.: www.hayhouse.co.uk
Published in India by: Hay House Publishers India: www.hayhouse.co.in

Cover design: Julie Davison
Interior design: Bryn Starr Best

**Library of Congress
Cataloging-in-Publication Data**

Names: Ludwig, Sandra Hinojosa, author.
Title: Chica, why not? : how to live with intention and manifest a life
    that loves you back / Sandra Hinojosa Ludwig.
Description: 1st edition. | Carlsbad, California : Hay House, Inc., [2021]
Identifiers: LCCN 2021000241 | ISBN 9781401959739 (trade paperback)
| ISBN   9781401959746 (ebook)
Subjects: LCSH: Self-realization in women. | Self-actualization
    (Psychology) in women. | Success.
Classification: LCC HQ1206 .L83 2021 | DDC 158.1082--dc23
LC record available at https://lccn.loc.gov/2021000241

Tradepaper ISBN: 978-1-4019-5973-9
e-book ISBN: 978-1-4019-5974-6

12 11 10 9 8 7 6 5 4
1st edition, April 2021

To Hobey, Diego,
Ximena, Iris, and Anna.

Sueñen en grande.

CONTENTS

INTRODUCTION

Y ou are holding in your hands my latest manifestation. One of my biggest, in fact. And it still feels surreal.

The chica who wrote this book seems at times so different from the chica who learned everything in this book through life experiences. Yet they are the same.

They are both the same girl with big brown eyes and mocha skin who grew up in Mexico thinking she was not enough. They are both the same determined adult with an accent who has lived around the world creating her own definition of success, and even though she didn't always know how to succeed, she never let that stop her.

When I think back to the girl who more than a decade ago was exhausted and beaten down by life yet felt a small glimmer of hope, I can't help but love her so much for it. She attracted everything that was needed for me to live the life I now live. She bravely confronted—and in fact continues to confront—her fears and pain so that I could be free. And I am so grateful to her. My story, which I share in this book, is unique, but at the same time probably not that different from yours.

Growing up I felt I was made for more. I felt there had to be a better way than what I knew. Through all my troubles, failures, and heartbreaks, I held on to the conviction that I deserved a better life and that finding the path toward it would be the beginning of it all for me. I suspect you have the same conviction, and it is my belief that picking up this book may be the beginning of the path for you as well.

Every step I took brought me here; every tear I cried was meant to form a river that would help me get downstream to my true happiness. Every turn I made that seemed to take me away from my dreams was meant to show me a new way I never imagined.

My life for the past 13 years has been one of blessings and growth. I not only have been able to manifest a life that truly loves me, but I have also been able to manifest the peace I have sought for so long. Although the road has had plenty of bumps, I have grown to have unshakable faith in the assistance of the Universe* and my ability to continuously raise my energy to a place where I am at my best to receive its support.

My life, like me, is not perfect, but it is beautiful in all its imperfection because of the strong connection I have been able to develop with my true self and with the Universe.

As I learned to shine my own light and reach out unapologetically for the life of my dreams, the people closest to me started doing the same. In fact, the idea of writing a book came from some of my closest friends: After I became their go-to person when they needed help striving to be their best selves, it helped me realize my love of helping others. This led to my becoming a life coach and launching my social media accounts through which I have now coached hundreds of Latinas and helped them gain the tools to reach for a life that loves them back.

---

*As you read this book, you will notice that I tend to refer to the Universe. This is my name for the higher power that works with us in our lives; it's my name for where we come from and where we will go to once we leave our place on Earth. It is the divine within us. Some people may call it God, Source, Spirit, etc. Use the name that feels best for you.

Six Steps to Creating a Life with Intention

Here is my promise to you: Everything you want is attainable, and it is easier to achieve than you think. Even though as a little girl you may have felt helpless to create the life you wanted, now as an adult you have the freedom to forge your own way and make the choices you need to make to create your reality. It is possible to avoid getting stuck in drama and despair every time you reach an obstacle. You can move with grace through the crappy times that sometimes happen while maintaining your clear intention and determination to create the life you want for yourself. It just takes knowing the right steps to make it happen.

I now share these steps with you, with the conviction that they can change your life as they have changed mine and the lives of countless other chicas who have learned them.

There are six steps that will be described in detail throughout the upcoming chapters in this book:

Create

Grow

Live with Intention

1. Clarity	2. Collaboration	3. Commitment

4. Curiosity

5. Compassion

6. Continuity

The first three steps—Clarity, Collaboration, and Commitment—are about creation. They help you bring into your reality anything you desire by teaching you the steps of the Law of Attraction and showing you how to use it intentionally to create the life that you want.

The last three steps—Curiosity, Compassion, and Continuity—are about growth. They help ensure the smoother ride in your life that I was referring to. Through my journey and the journey of the women I have met through my coaching practice, I have learned that although the first three steps manifest the desires in our hearts, skipping the last three steps is the reason why many times those great changes do not always last and why life continues to feel like an uphill battle even when we continue to manifest our goals effortlessly.

The first three steps are like painting and decorating your beautiful home, making it cozy and filling every corner with beautiful things, but the last three steps are about ensuring that the foundation of your home is strong and that the walls do not crack or come crashing down on you when a strong wind blows. Together they are the steps that create a life of intention that loves you back.

The first three steps are sequential, each step bringing you closer to manifesting your desires. The last three steps are tools you can bring in whenever you need help understanding and healing the fear and pain that will inevitably show up as you step into your light.

After all, living in the light may at times feel scary and overwhelming, and it demands from us that we go beyond our comfort zone and other people's ideas for our lives. ¡Chica, da miedo! (Girl, it's scary!)

Trust in the power and simplicity of the steps. They will help you navigate whatever comes up.

How This Book Is Organized

The first chapter of this book is where I share my life story and encourage you to reflect on your own life. The following chapters focus in turn on each of the six steps. Each chapter includes "¿Y Cómo?" ("And How?") exercises to help you understand and fully integrate the lessons, so you can move into the next step with full conviction that things are happening for you. I have tested these techniques myself as well as with hundreds of women in my coaching practice. I have seen them powerfully transform people's lives, so I know that they will help you gain confidence in the practicalities of applying each of the steps. Over time, these skills will become more than just words on a page; they will be an effortless part of your daily practice.

Each chapter will also address some of the "Sí, Pero" ("Yeah, But") stories we tell ourselves and use as excuses to avoid pursuing what we want. Knowing what these excuses are and being able to identify them will help you confront them as they arise in your life. Keep a blank journal handy for writing down your answers to the ¿Y Cómo? exercises as well as your reflections through the Sí, Pero sections. You can also download the worksheets as well as the pre-recorded guided meditations shared in this book at www.sandrahinojosaludwig.com/chicawhynot.

My intention is that this book will be the beginning of it all for you. Please know that a life that loves you back is possible. Not only that, it is also your right. You came into this world to create this amazing life for yourself. It's okay if you've failed before or were only mildly successful in the past. The life you want is within reach.

Now . . . ¡A darle con todo! (Give it your all!)

Chapter 1

An
UNINTENDED
Life

"Sandra, I feel like you gave up on life."

I stared at my friend Laura with a pained, questioning look. I didn't know what to say. In fact, I remained quiet for a while, as if the silence between us would make this feeling go away.

Those words seemed so foreign to me because that was not how I thought of myself. I wanted to tell Laura, "That's not at all how I feel! On the contrary! I feel exhausted after working my ass off day and night, trying to reach my dreams. I still want all of those things I dream about! I just don't know how . . ." I wanted to scream, cry, and have a hot churro with caramel filling dunked in hot chocolate all at the same time. I wanted to curl up in bed and wake up when I was a smarter person who knew how to win at this game called life. Instead, I said quietly, "I still want all of those things, I just don't know how to get them."

Let me back up a bit.

Laura is one of my closest friends. I'm not sure the exact instant we became friends, but I do know it was when I needed her the most. I was 22 and had just left my home in Monterrey, Mexico, to move to Querétaro, another area of Mexico, for a new entry-level role in a big food manufacturing company where Laura worked too. It was my first real job, but I saw it as so much more—as a chance to reinvent my life. I wanted to be so good at this job that the idea of it kept me up at night and pushed me to work late hours every day, including weekends.

I also badly wanted to build the life of my dreams. I wanted a boyfriend to share moments with, I wanted friendships that lit up my life, and I wanted money that would let me explore the world. Laura soon became my partner in crime as we both pursued similar dreams. Laura and I were part of a bigger group of friends we called "The Mob." The name had nothing to do with criminal activities, but with the fact that we all dressed as mob bosses for our company's Halloween party one year. The costumes included crazy dramatic makeup, suits, and cigars, so I guess it was the Mexican interpretation of what a mob would look like. They were the greatest group of friends. We had drinking parties on Wednesdays, when we would meet at Angelica's house, drink, and talk about work and boy problems while Cecilia built towers made out of beer cans. We also would go out on weekends to explore Acapulco, Mexico City, or Angangueo, to visit markets to eat tacos for breakfast, or to party at Señor Frog's or at the norteño music place where I once sang on stage on my birthday and ate tacos and drank tequila. We are still friends and talk often in our WhatsApp group.

Let's just say that in Querétaro I got the friends. I did not get the man, or the job I was really good at, or the money. But to this day, I am so grateful I got the friends.

When I was 25, however, I decided to try and reinvent myself . . . again. I became obsessed with realizing my life-long dream of studying in the U.S. When I was younger, *Beverly Hills, 90210* ran on Mexican television. I loved that show! The characters' lives seemed so complicated yet shiny, and I wanted to be those people. So I dedicated myself to acing both the English as a second language test and the science and engineering test that were required to get into a science master's program at a U.S. university. I worked my ass off for months.

The trigger for this renewed focus on my dream? A really bad relationship. I had gone to Querétaro in search of the life I had always hoped for myself, and instead I ended up with the life I so badly wanted to avoid. When you try to run from your problems without turning a critical eye on how you got there, you inevitably fall back into the same patterns again and again until you confront those ghosts from your past.

Ghosts from the Past

Let me back up to my childhood. I grew up in a house-hold with physical violence. In Mexican culture, it is not a strange thing for parents to give nalgadas (spankings) to their kids in an effort to discipline them. Some parents even dial up the pain element a bit by asking their kids to choose the weapon of choice: belt or chancla (sandal). I always chose chancla.

But the violence I lived with was worse than that. My dad also hit my mom. I still have memories of my dad in my early years. He was a good dad. He worked hard and provided for us. For him, education was so important, and he always made sure we had access to it. I even remember him bringing us sweet little things from his business trips when we were little and helping us pretend we were airplanes by lifting us with our stomachs on his legs while he lay in the floor.

But one day something shifted, and he became angry. He continued to provide for us, but he was no longer the same person. Soon after he started hitting my mom, he also started hitting my siblings and me. It was a "secret" everybody around us knew about.

The punishment was so brutal that those memories still haunt me to this day. The extreme violence started when I was 11 years old. At that time, as the oldest, I was often faced with the choice of hiding or defending my mom and siblings even though I knew it would bring me more blows. During this time, I felt very scared and lonely as the attention of the adults in our home shifted to my dad's anger. At that age I felt I needed to run away, yet I didn't dare do it without a plan. I needed to feel safe. It took me 10 more years to leave my house.

And yet, somehow, only four years after leaving home I found myself with an emotionally abusive boyfriend who one day pinned me against the wall and started screaming at me. I did not know how I ended up there. I was supposed to be a smart, professional woman. I was not supposed to walk in my mother's footsteps. Yet here I was, his face so close to mine that I could smell his breath and see the rage in his eyes. I thought he was going to punch me in the face. Yet, for reasons I don't know, he did not.

I could not stop thinking: *How did I get here?* The reason was that I was living an unintended life.

That was the moment I decided that I had to run away again and reinvent my life. And graduate school seemed like a good excuse to flee. After all, I was taught that "proper" Mexican women are not supposed to leave our families unless we are dressed in white or taken out feet first. So going away to study felt like a good excuse for me, an unmarried living Mexican.

I told myself I could do it; I was convinced of it. Obviously I had failed once, but surely I would not fail again. I had learned so much. I could have another go. I could make it work. I knew I could.

I could even work on becoming the girl my parents wanted me to be. Even though by then I had blown the "Mexican chica" expectations my family had for me, I knew if I tried one more time, I could at least meet some of them. Growing up, I was taught that all Mexican girls were born to marry by 25, have at least two kids by the time they were 30, cook amazing mole and tamales from scratch, and look the other way if they were unhappy in their marriage or in their life. I knew I could make it happen if I tried again.

And so, after I passed my exams, I applied to three American universities for graduate programs. They all accepted me, thanks to my lifelong dedication to my studies and having graduated with a chemical engineering degree from one of the best universities in Mexico.

When I went to say good-bye to my abuelito's (grandpa's) sister, she told me that I was making a mistake: "Men do not like smart women; you should get married first and then study whatever you want."

Regardless of my tía's prediction that I was about to ruin whatever chances I had for marriage, at age 25 I packed my 1994 red Chrysler with my clothes in a hamper, a lamp, and my dreams, and left Mexico to pursue my master's degree in the United States.

Little did I know this would become the theme of my adult life: running away to a new city, a new job, chasing a new life. As I was getting ready to run away from my life, Laura and I made a pact: We would visit each other once a year regardless of where we ended up in the world. To this day, we have kept this promise.

Years later, by the time Laura said that I had given up in life, I was 32 and had lived in four countries and seven cities. And my life did not look very different from when I was 25, except for the fact that now I had a shiny master's degree and lived in Toronto, Canada, and, according to my tía, I had no chance whatsoever of ever getting a man because I was too smart.

I was not about to give up, but I was starting to think that maybe my tía had a point. At 32, I was still pursuing bad relationship after bad relationship, none of which would last more than four months before they started falling apart.

In other areas of my life I was not any better, as I still worked like a desperate woman at jobs where I did not seem to get recognition or the promotion that I was so convinced I deserved. I made good money, but somehow it never lasted.

And my best friend, who knew all of my dreams, saw me not reaching any of them and thought I had given up in life.

I had not given up, though; I just did not know how to get what I wanted. It felt like I was spinning my wheels, and my race car would not move forward no matter what I did while everyone else around me was passing me on the racetrack.

I am so grateful to my friend Laura for those words, though. In retrospect, I know it must have been hard for her to say that to me, and I am forever in her debt. Although the words did not ring true initially, they highlighted a truth I had long avoided facing. I did not know how to do life. Ten years had passed from the first time I made a go at the life of my dreams, yet I was in the exact same place as before, just a different city. Surely there was a better way?

This conversation with Laura started my quest for understanding how life worked. What made successful people successful? What were they doing differently from me?

It was not long before the Universe started sending me clues, as it usually does when you find your voice, clearly express what you want, and focus on it.

"Calladita te ves más bonita" ("You look prettier silent") no more.

In 2006 I started therapy after realizing that it was not normal to cry nonstop while doing the dishes, or to get so triggered by telenovelas' sad episodes that I would cry myself to sleep. With the help of my new therapist, Elizabeth, I slowly started assembling the pieces of the puzzle that would become the foundation of this book. A chance encounter with the Law of Attraction that same year would then accelerate my understanding of how life works, and for once, I felt like my race car was starting to move.

What seemed so difficult for me to achieve was slowly starting to manifest in my life as a result of surrounding myself with great teachers, committing to being the best student possible, and experimenting with what worked and what didn't, what helped and what didn't.

By 2011, I had the husband, I had the house, and I had the promotion, including an international assignment.

Then there were the bonuses: I won a contest to be a torch-bearer for the Vancouver Olympics, I got Super Bowl tickets, an award at work, and even a $1,000 gift certificate.

I had finally found the how.

A Life with Intention

What I learned through those five years is that it is possible to build the life you want, and that life is not as complicated as we make it out to be; it just takes knowing the right steps and having the right attitude to make it happen. The difference between a life that does not feel like your own and a life that loves you back is intention.

A life with intention is a fully conscious life where all actions and thoughts are aligned to deliver to you what you seek. I am talking about the whole thing: your vision for your life, goals, thoughts, and actions, coupled with a profound self-knowledge that prevents you from making decisions or taking actions that are rooted in fear, other people's expectations, or cultural limitations.

It requires that we are brutally honest with ourselves about who we want to be as people and the kind of life we want for ourselves. It demands from us that we take responsibility for our choices and their consequences.

At all times in our lives we have two choices: get closer to or further away from what we want. Yet so many of us go through life like a leaf blown around by the wind, letting the driving force be the wind that decides where we end up. We either have no clarity about what we want, or we know what we want but don't live a life in accordance with it.

We let the relationships we experienced in our childhood shape what we expect of our future relationships or we date someone who will not be able to build with us the type of family we want. We let our economic situation, our ethnic background, or our nationality become obstacles that prevent us from reaching our goals, and we let our boss's mood dictate whether or not we will have a good day at work. We somehow decide that we will let everyone and everything around us tell us the kind of life we will have.

It's easy to give away our power because then we never have to look at our lives and realize it's mainly on us. Being responsible for our lives can feel scary, so instead we ask our family, our friends, or God to save us. We pray and wish someone would change something so we could finally be happy, and when they don't, we settle comfortably in the idea that our unintended life is not our fault. The issue with this, though, is that you get what others decide is best for you, and it's rarely what you wanted in the first place. And then you find yourself regretting the life you have and wishing you had done things differently.

It does not have to be this way. Within you is the power to move mountains: Trust me on this one. You have what it takes. You came here to shine a bright light. You came to thrive, not merely to survive.

Looking back now, I can see glimpses of genius in my life, when I became so committed to a goal that it was inevitable that I would reach it. When I decided to move to the U.S. to go to grad school, my English was not perfect and I did not have the perfect grade point average. I didn't even have money to pay for a move, let alone for school. I didn't know you could get paid as a research assistant. I just jumped, hoping there would be a net to catch me. After making it my goal to move, I just put one foot in front of the other and started walking down the path. I took the tests, I applied to the programs, and I got accepted. When I didn't know how to pay for it, the Universe put people in my path who had great advice about reaching out to professors asking for research or teaching positions. Soon enough, I found a professor who had money, but only for one year. I remember at the time the control freak in me felt this was too uncertain. Author William Paul Young says that when fear sets in, we either go to control or trust. It was a hard choice for me. My friend Luis told me to go for it, trusting that a path would appear before me. I did, and the path showed up. For as long as I was in school, I never had issues with funding.

I have many examples like this in my life, some of which I will share in this book, where trust in myself and in the Universe delivered to me what I wanted. But to do this, I had to let go of control, step out, face my vulnerability and fears, and do it anyway.

I know this will work for you as well. I have seen it time and time again in my life and the lives of people who have followed my teachings in my online community. You just need to make the decision to take the reins.

Once you decide to take ownership of your life by deciding who you want to be as a person and the kind of life you want to have, you will have clarity about what needs to get done. The steps to get there will soon become apparent. The Universe will conspire with you by sending you inspiration, people, events, and everything else you may need to get to your goal.

Fears will show up, but you will face them bravely and heal them along the way with compassion and determination. What you saw before as obstacles will now become valuable lessons that will show you the best way toward your dreams.

Once you are in this space, life will feel easier. The anxiety you constantly carry with you because you never know what will show up next in your life will fade away. Peace will take its place.

Even the way you speak to yourself will feel softer. Mistakes will provide the opportunity for learning and pivoting rather than berating and shaming. You will know that there is no wrong path, only paths that take you away from what you want, and the magic of this is that at any moment, you can just change paths back to your goals. You will know that the most loving thing you can do for yourself will be to create a support system made up of people who want to see you shine and whom you can call whenever you need help. And incidentally, as you shine your light, you will give others permission to shine theirs. You will change the world around you.

The hurt that you carry because of things in your past will no longer rule your life. You will be fully aware of your wounds and will tend to them lovingly, but you will not let your past keep you away from the future you so deserve.

You will finally cut yourself some slack and enjoy the present, instead of living in the prison of your past and the anxiety of the potential future. You will know that at any time, as your perspective shifts, you can change your mind about who you want to be and the life you want to live.

A Course in Miracles, a self-study system that aims to deliver spiritual transformation, says, "There is a way of living in the world that is not here, although it seems to be. You do not change appearance, though you smile more frequently. Your forehead is serene; your eyes are quiet.

And the ones who walk the world as you do recognize their own."

You will feel joy.

My intention is that this book will help turn your attention toward what is possible, just as Laura did for me. The life of your dreams is within reach. Not only that, it is your right. You came to this world to create this amazing life for yourself.

Go for it, chica! You deserve a life that loves you back! Make the decision now. Strap your boots on and start putting one foot in front of the other.

Because . . . chica, why not?

¿Y Cómo?

The Biography Exercise

Now, as you prepare yourself to go in depth into each of these steps, there is a first to take: writing your biography. Write this short biography as if you are looking back at all that you have achieved at the end of a long life, reflecting on the person you were and hoped to be. This will give you clarity in the present about what you ultimately hope for your life.

Start by finding a time when you will not be interrupted and a place where you can be by yourself. Decide at the beginning of this exercise that you will be honest—brutally honest—and true to your desires and dreams.

Grab your journal or some blank sheets of paper, and get ready to write. (If you'd prefer to take notes on your phone, computer, or other electronic device, that's fine too—whatever works for you!) I like to start the exercise with my clients by asking, "Who do you want to be when you grow up?" It reminds me that when we ask this question of kids, they never worry about how to make it happen. They dream big!

With this in mind, mentally step ahead far into the future. Then look back at your life as if all of your dreams had come true and describe who you have been as a person. Don't shy away from your big dreams. Go into detail. How have you lived your life? Who is the person you have become? What are the best memories your loved ones have of you? What did you accomplish in your career and in your community? What is the legacy you have built?

Now write details about your life. What are the highlights? What are the main values you have pursued throughout your life? How is your family life? What is your home like? What have you loved most? Try to go into as much detail as possible. This will be the vision for your new life.

If you start feeling fear or push back from the voices in your head saying things such as *How will you achieve this?* or *Who do you think you are?* remember, right now is not the time to come up with how you will make this happen. Just focus on what you have dreamed.

Once completed, save what you've written in a safe space and make it a habit to review it at least every six months. Rewrite it as needed as you get exposed to new perspectives and as your vision for your life changes. You wouldn't have the same vision of your life at 10 years old that you would have at 30.

There may be some things that will affect how you process the next steps. Your mind might put up resistance against this new way of thinking. It's normal; it's old programming, after all, and just giving it some light will make it slowly melt away and lead the way for a new perspective, or a miracle, as *A Course in Miracles* would call it.

Sí, Pero

- **"I can't because . . ."** Know that this voice will come up, and it will come up often. As you hear this little voice in your head when you read each of the steps, know that it is not your voice. It is one of the many voices that you heard when you were little that have become the recording that plays in your head, over and over. Sometimes it is the voice of our mamás blackmailing us into doing what the family expects of us, and sometimes it is the voice of our teachers telling us we are not smart enough. Sometimes it will be the voice of our abuelita (grandma) saying, "¿Pero qué dirán?" ("What will they say?"). It's okay; don't let those voices stop you. In Chapter 5 we will review these voices in depth, but for now, know they will be there.

- **"I have to be and do all of these things."** Growing up Mexican, I learned at an early age to ask too much of myself. After all, I had all of these expectations placed on me. I had to be smart, but not too smart. I had to be a great housewife, but look impeccable while cleaning the toilets, washing clothes by hand, and making tamales. I had to be pretty but be a niña bien (a good girl) and lower my eyes whenever a boy looked my way. I was given this set of standards that were impossible to meet. As you read this book, give yourself the space to be who you are and be honest when you can't do it all. It doesn't mean you can't have it all; it just means you may need to ask for help. It's okay; we were never meant to walk this path alone. Don't buy into the idea that you have to be perfect or that you have to ¡Ser fuerte, mijita! (Be strong, my daughter!). If you feel sad, seek help from a professional. If you feel tired, delegate, postpone, and take a nap. If you feel rushed, slow down and smell the roses.

- **"I want it now!"** If you are told that there is a way to have everything in your life, it is normal that you'll want everything to manifest now. But please do not fall into the trap of focusing only on stuff. As we walk through this book, you will see this process is so much more than about getting stuff, it is about creating a life of peace and joy that stays with you regardless of the circumstances of your life. It is about becoming the person you are meant to be and living the life you want for yourself. Be patient and trust in the Universe. Any other feeling besides trust is sending the energy of fear and doubt to the Universe. Relax. Breathe. And enjoy the ride.

Chapter 2

Step 1:
CLARITY

Define Your Bliss

"This is it! This is home!" I said to my sister as I walked around the beautiful house, touching the walls as if to make sure it was not a dream. I looked past the dining room into the beautiful pink kitchen and through the door that showed a small but beautifully landscaped backyard. I couldn't contain my emotion.

I was present in my now while visualizing the beautiful future I could build in this home. It was perfect. Not only because it was right in my price range and in the exact neighborhood I had dreamed of, but because it was exactly as I had dreamed. And when I say exactly, I mean it! Down to the color of the walls. It was love at first sight. I was home.

And I felt like I could finally exhale.

Let me back up a bit.

Owning a house had been a dream of mine since I first left my hometown. In Mexico, home ownership is the ultimate sign of stability, but for me it was a lot more than that. I had dreamed of a secure space I could call mine, where I could build my dreams and share the space with the husband and kids I did not yet have. It would be a place to entertain friends and for my loved ones to stay in when visiting from Mexico. After all, I had learned the art of hosting in my birth country. "De pared a pared es cama" ("Wall to wall is a bed") and "Le echamos más agua a los frijoles" ("We'll add more water to the beans") were some of the sayings I learned growing up. It's a personal offense if loved ones come to visit your town and don't stay with you.

This place would also be my sanctuary. It was a space full of light and love where I could sleep in peace knowing that I had nothing and no one to fear. A place where I called the shots. A place to call my home.

By the time I had found this home, I had been running from city to city, trying to start anew, to transform myself with every move, seeking safety. I had been moving every few years, never staying in a place long enough to call it home. I had become a nomad who had lived in 10 different addresses since I left my home in Monterrey 14 years before. I was tired, and I wanted a place where I could rest and build the life I wanted. For me this home meant rest, peace, and belonging. It was my future. It was my safe space.

I decided in 2007, a year after starting therapy and finding the Law of Attraction, that I would make my dream of owning a home happen. I decided to do something I had never done before—I wrote my dream down. With a pen and a notebook, I sat in the living room of my rented apartment, looking out the window to the homes across the street in my neighborhood that I loved, and I wrote down every single detail of my dream home:

> *It is a nice red-brick home, with an inviting porch and place to park my car off the street in a garage. It has a giant tree in the front, just like the houses I used to draw as a child. It has a beautiful open-concept living room–dining room with a fireplace and a kitchen that is well equipped. It also has a bathroom on the main floor.*
>
> *On the second floor it has a second bathroom and three bedrooms. It also has a finished basement where I have a TV room and a laundry room. It has a back-yard where I can sit at the end of the day to enjoy a cold drink.*
>
> *It is in my neighborhood of Bloor West Village in Toronto, Canada. It has yellow walls.*

After writing about my dream, I imagined how that home would be the safe space I had dreamed of and the place where the people I loved would make memories with me. I imagined my son or daughter growing up in this home, taking their first steps on its hardwood floors, and learning to ride their bike on those streets. Thinking about it would bring a smile to my face.

After I was done with the exercise of writing my dream, I folded the paper and kept it in my purse, looking at it often. This piece of paper was so precious I didn't dare part from it. I then started thinking about how to make it happen. I knew I had to get the Universe working for me. This was my chance to apply everything I had learned about the Law of Attraction in the previous 18 months. And as is the case, when you are very clear about what you want and you align your energy, the Universe wants nothing more than to bring it to you.

I got to work. I visualized with gusto, and I made sure to keep my energy high as often as was possible. I went on a diet from negative thoughts. I stopped reading and watching the news, and I became very careful about the people and situations I allowed in my life. I stopped with the chismes (gossip) and the drama and focused instead on things that made my heart sing.

I also put action into play. I moved from my lovely two-bedroom apartment near the subway to a small one-bedroom apartment far away from any public transport and without an air conditioner. This allowed me to save more money for my down payment, even if during the summer I had to sit outside to get some relief from the heat. The pay from any overtime I worked would go into my "awesome house" savings account. I went on a saving spree and learned how to invest for my down payment. And I did tons of research. I spent hours and hours understanding the market and the prices of homes. I became obsessed with a real estate website that showed all the new homes.

Soon the Universe came along showing me even more steps.

At the time, I was traveling every week for work for a new project on a new manufacturing line in Mississippi. A cat sitter would come and check on my cat, Smokey, every day, providing food and cuddles while I was away. One day upon my return, I noticed the card of a real estate agent on my dining room table with a note: "If you are ever looking for a home, give me a call." I took that card, smiled, and said, "Queeeeeé?" ("Whaaaaaat?"). Turns out my cat sitter couldn't make it that day, so she sent her mom, who happened to be an agent. She saw all of my real estate magazines and left that note. She turned out to be the agent who would find me my dream home.

Other things also started moving. My dad, out of the blue, decided to give me money to contribute to the down payment of my home. This was such an unexpected gift, and one that allowed me to expedite my goal of buying a home within about a year.

As I worked on securing my mortgage, the economy experienced an unfortunate collapse in 2008. I called my adviser immediately, worried about what this meant for my goals. To my relief, he confirmed that I could keep the interest rate that he'd previously quoted to me, even though rates had just increased by about 1 to 1.5 percent. I felt blessed to be given this opportunity to continue building upon my dreams during a time of such uncertainty and hardship.

It wasn't long after all these events that my real estate agent found the perfect property. My sister came to the showing, and when we walked in, I *knew* immediately. It was my home, down to the color of the walls. A few minor details were different, such as a bathroom on the main floor (although there was one in the basement) and a garage (it had a parking space off the street, though). But none of that changed my feeling of being home.

A couple of days later, I put in my offer. Even though it wasn't the highest offer, the owner, whom I had met during one of my visits, liked me. And that is how I bought my first home.

Having the clarity of what I wanted and also why I wanted it had helped me maintain my energy and allowed the Universe to pleasantly surprise me with ways that made acquiring my home almost effortless.

I had discovered the power of clarity.

The Power of Clarity

Everything starts with knowing what you want. Want to go shopping? The store that you choose will depend on what you are hoping to buy. Going to a place you have never been before? You need to know the destination in order to get a map. Want to cook something tonight? You need to know what you will be cooking in order to make sure you have all the ingredients.

When you don't have clarity about what you want, it's impossible to live an intentional life. Clarity is like the glass in a prism, which when combined with the sun produces those gorgeous color reflections on every surface it shines on. Without clarity, the sun, which in this case is the Universe, cannot deliver on the beauty that we seek. It still brings its light to our life, but in a more general way that continues to provide well-being without specifically delivering the beautiful colors that will make our life rich and enchanting, and without the individual hues that will make our heart sing and move our energy forward.

Without clarity our world is dull.

When we have clarity in our life, it becomes a laser-focused energy that allows the Universe to become our manifestation partner. The Universe then rearranges the world to bring that desire to us while also giving us inspiration for the actions we need to take to get us closer to what we want. (More on that in the next chapter.)

Clarity also allows our energy to remain certain and at a high vibration. Lack of clarity, on the other hand, feels like frustration and keeps our energy stuck. Clarity is the channel that allows energy to flow between us and the Universe.

Yet it seems that clarity is never the first step in our journey of co-creation with the Universe. We decide that things need to move, and we are too busy to stop and reflect. We decide we will figure out the rest later, including what we really want. We get confused about the source of our desire, and sometimes we allow others to set the pace of what we are working toward.

Before we know it, we are frantically moving toward something we didn't want in the first place—most of the time quite unconsciously.

Generating clarity is a two-step process. First you start with the *what* of your desire, and then you proceed to the *why*, the reason you want that desire.

The *when*, the *how*, the *where*, and the *who* are the business of the Universe, and although it's okay to put some thought into it, putting too much emphasis on these four questions could generate resistance within us that makes us focus on the future with anxiety and not allow the Universe to work its magic. That is why *clarity* stands for *what* and *why*.

The what is generated when we are living and observing our day-to-day lives and come up with the inspiration that something could be different, better, bigger, shinier. That realization is the seed of the what.

The what can sometimes hit us all at once, like a light bulb flashing on in a millisecond when the desire is immediately revealed in our minds. We live as normal in a situation and then immediately know what we would like to be experiencing instead.

Other times, the what blooms slowly within us, like a flower that takes its time to grow and become known. The same way that it can be hard to recognize which flower will bloom from a bud, we can also sometimes get confused about what it is that we want. We know that we want something different from what we are living, but we may not know yet what it is. It takes patience to allow that flower to grow and reveal its color, shape, and aroma.

In a world of immediate gratification, many times we don't allow our desire to bloom, and instead look around for clues about what it may be. We look at things we don't want, and we put our energy there, or we look at things others want, and we put our energy there.

There are times when we are clear on what we want, but we either don't dare dream it for fear that it may not be possible, for fear of what others may say, or because it's just too scary to leave the world we know to pursue the world we hope for ourselves. And then we shove our dreams down and pretend they do not exist. We betray ourselves by not acknowledging our voice. We live in a facade of what we think is safe.

Regret is made of dreams we didn't pursue.

The issue, though, is that if you are thirsty, only water will do. But because we are so uncomfortable waiting for the answer or living our truth, we take anything that just looks like water and think it may quench our thirst.

This causes confusion, frustration, remorse, and wasted work. We become obsessed with creating something that is not what our soul is asking from us, and when our soul tries to show us the way to what it really wants, immediately we tell it, "Stop, don't you see I am busy?"

Life becomes a rat race that takes us nowhere. We find ourselves running toward the wrong destination. We lose the compass of our desire and our life reflects that. We become like a leaf being dragged from one place to another by the wind, with no real say on where it may end up.

Defining Your What

Having clarity in our desires is an exercise on removing confusion and uncertainty. It is an exercise of self-reflection and honesty. A clear *what* has all of the following:

1. INTEGRITY

Your desire is in alignment with the person you want to become and the life you want to lead. In the previous chapter's exercise, you wrote what you hope for your life in the form of a short biography. This is the bigger picture of the life you hope to live. You know your desire is true to the life you want to live when it gets you closer to that picture. If, instead, your desire is taking you away from your overall vision of your life, chances are that you are letting something or someone else other than your true self take charge of your life planning or you are letting confusion set in and cloud your judgment. In both cases a quick check-in with your overall vision for your life will return you to center.

2. AUTHENTICITY

Within this pillar you connect deeply with yourself. Your desire is in alignment with the core part of you, and not with the wounded part of you that gets easily triggered or that makes you freeze. The wounded part of you is the one where your fears live, and the one that sometimes drives you to do things that are not in alignment with who you really are.

You find yourself with an urge to change or do something in your life because of your fear. You can also find yourself paralyzed because of it and decide not to pursue your dreams, as it feels safer to stay put. Fear can manifest as such, or in any of its disguises, such as sadness, anger, etc. More on these disguises in Step 4.

When you are not living from a place of authenticity, you may do things such as staying in a toxic relationship to feel less lonely or avoid "El qué dirán" ("What would people say"); you find yourself losing control and losing your temper with someone because they are annoying you with something that sounds too close to the truth and you want them to stop.

You may also have a fear of confronting someone in your life such as your mamá or your amigos. You don't want to reveal your true self and your true thoughts for fear of losing them, hence you create a mask for every occasion that results in you acting according to it.

When your what is authentic, it comes from love and it feels good to think about it. It uses words such as *like* and *love*. If, however, you feel any kind of anxiety or urgency around it and see yourself using words such as *should, must,* and *need,* and the thought of it not manifesting is your worst nightmare, chances are that it is rooted in fear. Step 4: Curiosity will help you have a clearer view of what is behind the fear that prevents you from being your true self.

3. POSITIVITY

Your desire is connected to what you want, not to what you don't want. It seems like such a simple thing, but focusing on what you want is so important. The Universe responds to your energy, and when you focus on what you don't want, that is where your energy lives and is exactly what the Universe responds to. So, for example, instead of saying "I don't want to be sick," say "I want to be healthy";

instead of saying "I don't want to be poor," say "I want to be abundant."

This gives a clear directive to the Universe, allowing it to respond in kind.

This is also something to consider in your day-to-day language. Everything you speak and think becomes your point of attraction. The Bible says, "The mouth speaks of what the heart is full of," and that means that if you are focusing on "I don't want to be sick," sickness is what is in your heart and your vibration.

When you change the tune, the dance changes as well.

4. SPECIFICITY

The Universe's answers tend to be more precise when you are specific about what you want. Yet many times you may latch on to very general thoughts. The most common one is "I want to be happy." What does that even mean, mija?

It's no different than going to a restaurant and telling the server that you want "food" when they come to take your order. They will look at you, question your sanity, and bring you braised lamb when what you wanted were tacos.

When you are not specific, you risk getting something you totally didn't want.

DEFINING YOUR WHY

Once you have a *what* with integrity, authenticity, positivity, and specificity, you now need to take it one step further and ask yourself, *Why?*

This is the real magic sauce, and more will be explained in the next chapter. But for now, the why is the reason behind your desire. It is what is at the core of the wish that you have. It's the engine behind your hope for things to be different.

We all want something because we think it will make our lives better, but understanding what "better" means for us is the way to identify the why.

For example, if you want a bigger house, knowing how that bigger house will make your life better is your why. It could be because you want a safe space where all of your family members have a place they can call their own. It could be that you want a home where you can entertain your loved ones and have pachangas (parties) that will create happy memories for all.

There may be another side of the coin, where you realize your why is tied to things or people outside yourself. For example, you may find you want a bigger house to impress your family, or to show those mean kids from high school that you are much better than all of them.

If this is your why, go back and connect yourself with who you really are, and stop living your life for others. When you live for others, you not only end up resenting them, you also lose your capacity to create the life that you want and deserve because you are so focused on what Juan or Isabel will say.

And not only are you wasting your time—because I can assure you Juan over there is giving you very little thought—but you are also wasting your life, your one precious life, by not being true to yourself.

Focusing on identifying your why is the ultimate test of honesty and authenticity. In addition to validating your desire, focusing on the why helps with manifestation. As it will be explained in the next chapter, it helps focus your energy while giving the Universe the chance to surprise you and deliver your desire in ways you never thought possible. Ignoring the why gives the Universe a very narrow set of parameters that may or may not address the reason behind your wish.

Years ago, I thought I was ready to get engaged to my boyfriend. I was new to the Law of Attraction and was ready to make it happen for me, so I started visualizing a ring (my what). I would think about the size of the ring, the sparkle of it, the weight of it. I would picture the ring because I thought that was how I was going to manifest it.

After doing this for a while, I went on a business trip to Chicago. I was attending a massive conference, and the line for the taxis was miles long. Looking at my options, I decided to walk back to my hotel. It was an hour walk, but the day was beautiful along the lakeshore, and I was up for it, so I started walking at a slow pace, enjoying the afternoon sunshine.

A few minutes into my walk, I saw something sparkling on the sidewalk ahead of me. Curious, I picked up the pace to see what it was. As I got closer, I realized it was a ring! A sparkly, shiny, beautiful ring.

In that moment, I realized the Universe had a sense of humor. I picked up the ring and looked up to the sky, and with a smile on my face, I said out loud to the Universe, "This is not what I had in mind!"

I had no why, and by focusing only on the what, the Universe gave me exactly that! I bet it had a chuckle along the way too.

After that, I started focusing on my why.

The what and the why are the beginning of the manifestation process and the root of living a life with intention. The following exercises will help you make sure you are able to identify them.

¿Y Cómo?

Bubble Exercise

The objective of this exercise is to map out each area of your life as it is right now. Once you complete it, you will find it easier to focus on one area to work on. When you focus on a single area, the Universe starts to deliver on it while also rearranging itself to deliver all of your other desires, as long as they are in your vibration. After all, aligning your energy is the wind that pushes all sails, as long as they are facing the right way. Also, focusing on one area, especially at the beginning, allows you to reacquaint yourself with the fantastic creator that you are while building your confidence. The area you pick could be whatever you feel is closest to your heart. It could be something small or something a bit bigger. It is up to you.

Start by finding a time when you will not be interrupted and a place where you can be by yourself. Decide at the beginning of this exercise that you will be honest—brutally honest. Do a thorough inventory of your life as it is right now. It will help you to see it all on paper.

To complete this exercise, use the following diagram to get you started. You can download a template for this and many other exercises at www.sandrahinojosaludwig.com/chicawhynot.

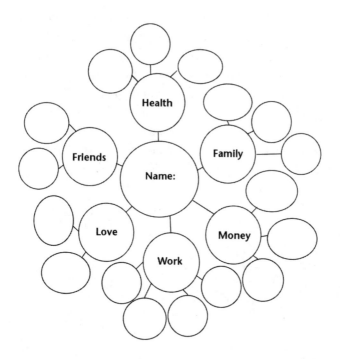

Start by writing your name in the circle in the middle. Now in each bubble around that main circle with your name, fill in the areas that you feel are the most important in your life at this moment. I have gotten you started by including health, family, money, work, and love. Create as many more bubbles as you need. Then, for each of these categories, use the secondary bubbles to describe how your life is right now. Include positive aspects as well as not so positive aspects. For example, connected to money you may have one bubble that says "I don't make enough money," or "I have to support my younger siblings," or "I have $30,000 in debt," or "My mom gives me a $500 stipend every month to help make ends meet." Then, if necessary, draw more bubbles that will branch out from those aspects. For example, you may add bubbles connected to "I have $30,000 in debt" that say "I spend more than I make," "I have to use my credit card for emergencies," "It is a low-interest debt," or "It has not increased for the last five years." Create as many bubbles as you need to complete the map of your life as it is right now.

Here is an example:

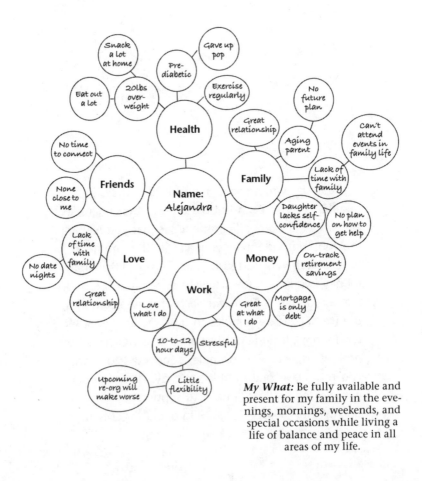

My What: Be fully available and present for my family in the evenings, mornings, weekends, and special occasions while living a life of balance and peace in all areas of my life.

Once you are finished, look at the map you've created. This is your life as it is. The good, the bad, and the ugly. Look at all the areas that seem to pull at your heartstrings the most, the ones that you feel more inspired to improve. Be open to the possibility that the area that worries you the most may require that other areas improve first, and you might have to start there. For instance, in the previous example, if you started this exercise worried about your daughter's lack of self-confidence, you may realize through the exercise that even if you want to help, you do not have time to do it because your job takes up most of your energy. In this case, step one may be finding a new job where you have more free time to be present for your family. So that may be the area you decide to work on.

Once you select an area to work on, you can (1) write a statement for your what as it relates to that area of your life, or (2) take that area and expand on it more in the Magic Wand Exercise that follows if you have trouble coming to a what right now.

If you decide to write the what, do so at the bottom of the page, under the bubbles, and verify its integrity, authenticity, positivity, and specificity as explained in this chapter. Adjust as needed or pick a new area if you find it fails in any of the ways listed above.

The Tree Exercise

The objective of this exercise is to help you with specificity for your what. In my practice, I have seen people who are unable to articulate their what beyond "I want to be happy." This exercise helps to flesh out what that means and select a specific area to focus on.

Start by finding a time when you will not be interrupted and a place where you can be by yourself. Decide at the beginning of this exercise that you will be honest—brutally honest. Really dig deep and answer what each of the statements in the trunk and the limbs of the tree means for you. Allow yourself the space to be sincere.

If you start feeling fear or pushback from the voices in your head because they are saying things such as *How will you achieve this?* or *Who do you think you are?* remember, right now is not the time to come up with how you will make this happen. Just focus on what you have dreamed. All of it.

To complete this exercise, use the following diagram to help you get started. You can download the template for this exercise at www.sandrahinojosa ludwig.com/chicawhynot.

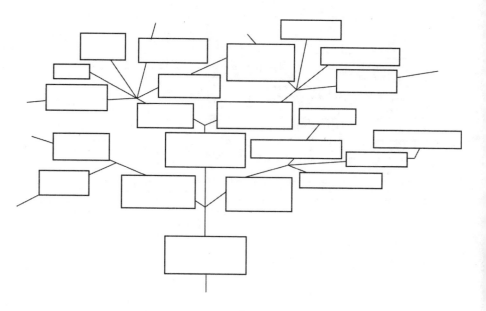

Start by writing your general thought in the trunk. It could be something like "I want to be happy," or "I want to be rich." Now write down in the boxes in each of the limbs a little more about what "being happy" or "being rich" means to you by asking yourself, what does this mean for me? Create as many limbs and boxes as needed, each time asking yourself, what does this mean for me? If the boxes are still too general, continue drawing limbs, asking yourself each time, what does this mean for me? Continue until you get to more concrete desires around that topic.

The following is one example of how someone might fill out the boxes:

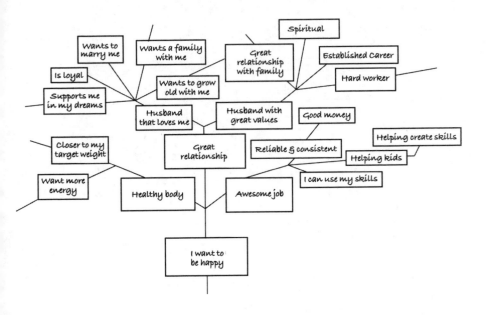

My What: A great marriage with a partner that loves me, wants a family, is loyal, is supportive of my dreams, and grows old with me

Once you have completed your tree, pick an area of focus and articulate your what. If this proves to be a bit difficult, move to the Magic Wand Exercise below. For example, in the tree above, the person may realize that one of the big areas that will make her happy is having a partner who meets all of the criteria she outlined. She may pick that to be her area of focus.

If you decide to write the what, do so at the bottom of the page, under the tree, then verify its integrity, authenticity, positivity, and specificity as explained in this chapter. Adjust or pick a new area as needed.

The Magic Wand Exercise

The objective of this exercise is to allow you to drop some of your resistance around an area and instead indulge fully in your dreams while further refining your what. It's about giving your dreams the space to fully exist as they come.

Start by finding a time when you will not be interrupted and a place where you can be by yourself. Decide at the beginning of this exercise that you will be honest and allow yourself to dream as big as you possibly can. Also, allow yourself to ignore the voices in your head that will inevitably come up: *Who do you think you are?*; *You are not smart enough*; *You don't have the money to do this*; *Your mamá will be hurt if you do that*; *Las tías will never stop talking about me if I do that*; or *People like me never achieve things like that.*

Find a comfortable spot to sit. Settle on a couch or a pillow on the floor, with paper and pen. Take a deep breath and close your eyes. Give yourself a couple of minutes to focus solely on your breath and the quiet around you. Now imagine that your best version of a fairy godmother comes to you and asks you what you want. Out loud, say the area of your life you've chosen from either the Bubble Exercise or the Tree Exercise, and imagine the fairy godmother tapping you gently on your head with her magic wand. Now anything and everything you ever wanted is possible. Anything you desire is yours without having to worry about the when, how, who, or where.

All that you want comes instantly without you even moving a finger.

Now start witnessing your desire coming true. What does it look like? Focus on all the details as they come alive. Focus on the feelings of happiness that come with having all of your wishes fulfilled, making your stomach sing with butterflies. Enjoy this space for as long as you want. If your mind brings a complaint about the feasibility of your dream, let it float away just like a cloud moves across the sky, and continue to focus on your delicious creation.

Once you are ready, open your eyes. Write down everything that you saw. Include every detail you can remember, from the weather to your clothes to the sensations and feelings you experienced. Record it all in present tense. Now read it out loud and enjoy the clarity.

The Why Exercise

The objective of this exercise is to allow you to articulate the why behind your desire. It will also help you verify the integrity and authenticity of your desire by digging deeper into the roots of it. This exercise is the foundation for Step 2: Collaboration, as described in the next chapter.

Start by finding a time when you will not be interrupted and a place where you can be by yourself. Decide at the beginning of this exercise that you will be honest—brutally honest. This is an exercise between you and the Universe, so allow yourself to really articulate the intentions behind your desire.

Find a comfortable spot to sit. Take a deep breath and close your eyes. Visualize a movie screen in front of you. See your wish becoming a movie in which you are experiencing exactly what you wanted. As you are watching it on the screen, ask yourself, *Why do I want this?* Focus on the you in the screen. What is the feeling that the you in the screen is experiencing? Pride, happiness, achievement, peace? Now try to discern pride in what, or happiness about what, or achievement for having reached what, or peace about what?

Start listening for those answers. Some of the answers may look like this:

- I want the big house because I want to feel the pride of providing for my family and experiencing my family being in their own space.

- I want the promotion because I want the happiness of seeing myself grow from an individual contributor to a manager, where I can experience the pride of achieving my long-lasting dream while also having the peace of having more say in the direction in which the company will go.

- I want the husband because I want the happiness of creating my own family, a place where I belong, and a partner who stands by my side as we support each other's visions for our lives. I want us to experience the joy of having our own kids and seeing them grow.

This is your why, the heart of your desire. Enjoy it. Just like cleaning the leftover mole on your plate with your tortilla is the most enjoyable part of the meal, so is coming up with the why.

Now, if through this process you find that your why comes from a wounded place, such as "I want to impress others" or "I want to show all the haters," or comes from wanting to please others—"So my mamá can be happy" or "So my tías stop bothering me at funerals about when I am going to get married"— take a pause. This is great! You have now verified that your desire is not integral (it is not in alignment with what *you* want for *your* overall life) or authentic (it does not come from *your* core self; instead, it comes from your fears). Go back to your Bubble Exercise or your Tree Exercise and review it again. Did you answer honestly from your core, or from your wounded self? Repeat the exercises as needed to gain clarity about what *you* really want, independently of what others may want, and without letting your fear take over.

When you allow your desire to come from a wounded place, the risk is that no matter what you do, you will never fulfill your desire to be happy. Fear tells you stories about what you need, but it never really addresses the main pain, which may be that you are feeling that you are not loved or that you aren't deserving. The things you may be reaching for may not be able to provide what you need, which is to connect with your core self.

If you want to further explore the fear behind this slight detour, go to Step 4: Curiosity before attempting the exercises again. It will help you to overcome the fear and go into your true self.

Sí, Pero

- **"Even after doing all the exercises, I can't come up with what I want."** If this is happening, chances are that you have some significant resistance around your dreams. Be gentle with yourself. When we push down our desires for years because wishing may be more painful than staying where we are, it just becomes second nature to push away what we truly want. I recommend exploring this in Step 4: Curiosity. If the resistance is too much, seek the help of someone who can gently guide you through exploring this part of you. Nothing is lost; nothing is broken. You may just need some guidance into getting in contact with your true self. A fantastic therapist or a coach will help you do just that.

- **"I want this, but my family wants that."** We all love our families, and if, like me, you grew up in a Latino family, chances are you have a great deal of loyalty and respect for them. However, pursuing your dreams in no way disrespects your family or makes you disloyal. On the contrary, your ability to dream and your strong desire to pursue dreams is a testament to the human being they raised. If you still are afraid of your family suffering because of your decisions, know that their choice to suffer is their reaction to their own fears. Acknowledge their fears and have compassion for them—but do not try to change them, because you can't. And whatever you do, do not adopt their fears as your own. Living your life to the fullest is the best thing you can do for yourself and for them. Shining your light at its brightest gives them permission to shine their own. Above all, remember that they love you, and it may take time for them to come to terms with your vision for your life, which may be different from their vision for their life.

- **"I don't know how things will unfold, so I don't dare to dream big until I have all the details of the *how*."** If you have relied on yourself for a long time, it's normal to want to control the outcome. It's scary to let go and trust that the Universe has your best interest at heart and will deliver to you exactly what you want. But in this case, trusting is a lesson we all have to learn. If trusting in big things such as meeting a husband or getting the promotion feels too scary, start with something smaller, such as buying the pillow of your dreams, or finding the shoes you have been dreaming of. As you continue to strengthen your manifestation muscle, you will realize what an amazing creator you are and what a great partner you have in the Universe. Once you come to this realization, you will start daring to have bigger and bigger dreams, with the certainty that the Universe is always working for you. Remember that dreams are whispers from the Universe of what is possible in your life. Do not doubt it can happen for you.

- **"I realize now my *why* is to impress others."** If this is your why, become very curious about it and try to understand which fear is at the root of wanting to impress others. Step 4: Curiosity will be a great ally in understanding this. Once you bring your fear to the surface, you will have the freedom to go back with a stronger connection to yourself and reframe your what. Continue to verify your what for its integrity, authenticity, positivity, and specificity. The clarity exercise is about giving yourself the space to be honest with yourself while also strengthening the connection to your core self. It is all about you.

Chapter 3

Step 2:
COLLABORATION

Let the Universe
Be Your Concierge

". . . and then one day, he stopped complaining. Four years later he was the president of our company."

I listened to my drunken colleague slurring next to me in the back of a Nissan. What he had just said about our newly minted company president made the hair on my arms stand up and my brain start going 100 miles a minute.

It was February 2006, and we had just attended our company's annual meeting. This day included an event where we reviewed the company strategy, followed by a party to celebrate our wins. I had decided to take public transit so I could fully participate in the festivities without any worries. However, while the meeting was downtown, where public transit is readily available, the party turned out to be on the other side of the city. The company provided shuttles for the 40-minute trip, but I knew it would be hard taking transit back from there to my apartment. I decided to cross that bridge when the time came and enjoy the party.

There was dancing, there was singing, and there was alcohol. And apparently my colleague, the director of finance, also enjoyed it very much.

When the party ended, I had to find a way to get home. I knew a taxi would cost un ojo de la cara (an eye from my face), so I started asking my colleagues for a ride. A woman from human resources offered to share her car with me. She was driving to a club downtown where the party would continue, and I could easily get home from there. I jumped in the car, along with three other colleagues who were excited to go to the club. That's how I found myself sitting next to my wild-haired, reeking-of-alcohol colleague.

On the way to the club, he started telling us how nice the new president of the company was. Apparently, he was a big fan. He kept saying "He is *so* nice. He is *soooo* nice. He is *suuuch* a *nice guy.*" As he noticed that we started losing interest in his declaration of love for our new boss, he started to add more dimension to the story by telling us about the president's beginnings. He told us he had started a few years back as a junior marketing manager in the company. According to him, the new president used to "complain about absolutely everything. He complained about the projects he had, the projects he didn't have, the people he had to work with, and the people he didn't have to work with." And that's when my drunken colleague said the words that would forever change my life ". . . and then one day he stopped complaining, and four years later he was the president of our company."

I looked at him without knowing what to say or what his words would mean in my life. But I knew that I'd just been given a gem.

Let me back up a bit.

At the time I heard my colleague tell us this story, I was a frustrated quality assurance technician in my company, with dreams of becoming a product developer and getting promoted. I worked hard; in fact, I was working the hardest I had ever worked in my life. I would work from 8 A.M. to 8 P.M. most weekdays, adding more hours during the weekend. Yet I couldn't make a promotion happen. I saw people around me getting the promotions I thought I deserved and people with far less experience than me being hired into higher jobs. I had run out of ideas on what to do to be seen and recognized. I was angry and bitter about that, and my day-to-day demeanor showed it.

So when my colleague told me that story, I saw myself in that tale. The truth is, I complained a lot. In fact, I was kind of known for complaining. I decided to keep this story in my mind and try to figure out what to do with it. Soon the Universe would show me the next steps.

Not long after this event, I was working from home. This was 2006, so working from home was not really a thing back then, but for whatever weird reason, I was working from home that day. Even stranger is the fact that I was a quality assurance technician for a manufacturing plant. QA technicians work on the line. I have no idea why I was able to work from home, but the Universe did.

Even though I was working, I had the TV on for background noise. Since ordinarily I was not home during the daytime, and this was way before the DVR era, it felt so luxurious to listen to daytime television. So I did. And my show of choice was, of course, *The Oprah Winfrey Show*.

That day her guests were from the movie *The Secret*. I had never heard of that movie, but it sounded interesting. As I worked, I heard the guests explain that we all have the ability to create our own reality. That seemed to me a little crazy, but wasn't that what the president of the company had done? I stopped my work and listened more intently. I was intrigued.

As soon as I was done with work, I had to see that movie. I went back to my computer and started looking frantically for the movie on the Internet and luckily found a version on YouTube. At the time, I didn't realize that I was watching the first version of the movie. (The movie was edited to remove many scenes, and this revised version is the one that became popular and the one that is currently distributed.) I heard all kinds of speakers, coaches, and authors describe this universal energy that creates worlds, and how we can align our energy through gratitude and other good-feeling thoughts to bring to us what we desire. Just like that. They called it the Law of Attraction. It sounded like magic.

I was especially fascinated by one author in particular: Esther Hicks, who appeared only in this original version of the movie. Her description of the Law was so easy to understand, and her advice to apply it seemed so practical. I decided I had to learn more.

I spent the whole night looking through her website. I discovered that she channeled a group of entities called Abraham, and that Esther, together with her husband, Jerry, had been teaching the Law for many years. I read their quotes, I listened to their recordings, and I noticed they had a book called *Ask and It Is Given*. I got that book soon after.

I also noticed they did live events. To my surprise, Esther and Jerry would be in my town just a couple of weeks later for a weekend workshop, starting on March 17. My heart exploded. And within minutes, I had a ticket.

I arrived early on the first day of the workshop, sat at the front, and listened to Esther speak and answer questions all weekend. I took notes como si no hubiera un mañana (as if there were no tomorrow), not wanting to miss a single detail. I learned all about contrast and rockets of desire and how to ride the rocket. I came alive. I couldn't believe this Law was a thing I never knew about. How was it possible that I was in my 30s and I didn't know this was a thing?

When I got home, I was a changed person. I typed all of my notes into a document and shared it with as many people as I knew. I continued to learn. I signed up for Esther and Jerry's CD subscription, and every month I got a new CD with more teachings. I listened to them nonstop every time I got in my car.

But more important, I put everything I learned into practice. I stopped watching news, as well as scary and sad movies, since I noticed those lowered my energy. I stopped looking at the negative aspects of my life and focused only on the positive aspects. I became protective about my energy and my space and allowed people to come close to me only if they helped me maintain it.

Soon my colleagues at work started noticing the changes. I even had a human resources person, who had in the past given me feedback about my behavior, stop me and ask what was different about me.

Things started manifesting into my experience. I got an opportunity to work on a product development project in Thailand, and then I got moved from my role into a higher-level job to cover a leave. I was then moved to one of the biggest new product launches for my company as the lead developer, followed by another move 11 months later to my coveted promotion as product development manager.

Everything I had desired was now coming to me.

I still remember the first day I walked into the meeting room with the door marked Leadership Team Meeting. I had such a feeling of gratitude and happiness.

I quickly started seeing manifestations beyond my career, and within five years I had a fantastic house, a loving husband, and an overseas assignment. I even won a spot carrying the Olympic torch for the 2010 Winter Olympics in Vancouver.

I had found the *how*.

The Law of Attraction

The Law of Attraction is the universal law that says that everything that exists first started as thought. It is a law just like the law of gravity that keeps our feet on the ground or the law of conservation that tells us that neither matter nor energy is created or destroyed, only transformed.

We don't need to think about these laws to make them happen—they just happen. They are always reliable. We wake up and our feet hit the ground, whether we like it or not, because of the law of gravity. This law keeps cars on the roads, makes apples fall from the trees, and ensures amazing Olympic divers hit the pool every time. It is consistent, meaning it is always true. We may not be able to predict who will win the next soccer World Cup, but we can always be sure that gravity is working for us.

The Universe takes care of all of this for us. It is the same with the Law of Attraction. It is always happening. The Law tells us that everything has a vibration. The Universe's natural vibration is the highest there is. This is the overall vibration of well-being.

All of our thoughts also have a vibration. When this vibration is closely aligned with the energy of the Universe, we let all of the well-being of the Universe flow to us. When the vibration is not closely aligned, we prevent all of that well-from being from coming to us as fast as it could. Our alignment is like the water tap: When it's on, water pours out; when it's not, water stays in the pipe. It's all within us. The ability to manifest the world we want is within us.

These are the steps to bring the Law of Attraction into practice:

STEP 1: ASK

This step happens unconsciously. When something happens in your life that is not 100 percent to your liking, a thought emerges in your mind that says it would be better if something were different. You may not have the whole answer of what "different" might look like, but you know something different is needed. That is the act of asking from the Universe.

Over time, you may add more definition to the desire, but for now your energy is one of asking. And that is enough for the Universe to get to work.

Your asks change over time. Right now, you may think an amazing sequined dress would be chingón (super cool), and tomorrow when fashion changes you may think a little black dress would be increíble (awesome). Your asks are always evolving and changing depending on what is in front of you and where you are in life. What you want when you are 20 will be different from when you are 40 and will be different from when you are 60 or 80. Your current circumstances give you a specific view on things, and your asks change as you change. Life causes you to ask.

In the previous chapter, I explained in detail how to achieve clarity for what you want, so use that clarity to ask for exactly what you want.

STEP 2: MANIFEST

Once you ask, the Universe gets to work immediately, just like a concierge attending to your every wish. It creates a perfect solution for your ask. Now your job is to attract it into your life and make it real. This act is called manifestation.

The way to manifest what you want is by aligning your energy closely to the energy of your desire. And since your desire is something that would make you happy, it is of a high vibration, meaning your vibration to manifest it must be as high.

Sometimes you might think, *How can I be happy now? I will be happy when I get my desire.* But that's not how the Law works. You need to be happy now to attract what you desire, because a matching vibration is what brings your desire into existence.

In order to make your vibration high, make feeling good your priority. Feelings are a great indicator of where your thoughts are. That means that when you feel good, your thoughts are of high vibration, and when you feel bad, your thoughts are of a lower vibration. Monitoring your thoughts would be impossible, as you have way too many thoughts, so focusing on feelings is the best way to assess what you are thinking about. When you are thinking thoughts that get you closer to what you want, you feel good. So, the key is to feel good during your day as much as you can.

Become obsessed with feeling good. Some things that may help you feel good include:

- **Avoid watching news or seeing scary movies.** They make you have lower vibration feelings, such as sadness, anger, or frustration, which makes them not the best use of your time. Dedicate your time instead to reading or watching material that makes you feel good, makes you laugh, and helps you see the best in life.

- **Avoid people who continuously bring chisme (gossip) and drama into your life.** Do not allow people into your space who will cause you to lower your energy. Over time, you will learn how to live with these people while maintaining control of your vibration, but if you are a beginner with the Law of Attraction, try to avoid them altogether. Instead, surround yourself with people who celebrate you as a person and who make gratitude their daily prayer. If you don't have many people like that around you right now, don't worry, as you change your energy, people of the same vibration will start appearing in your life because of the Law of Attraction.

- **Dedicate time to activities that make your heart sing.** Activities such as dancing, gardening, fishing, yoga, massage therapy, spending time with loved ones, and eating foods that favor your body—in other words, *anything* that makes you feel good—are of high vibration. If you have to do activities that you do not look forward to, such as changing the oil in your car or washing the dishes, look for ways to make those activities more enjoyable by listening to an uplifting audiobook, listening to music, or doing the activity with a loved one.

- **Visualize what you want and the feeling of having it right now.** When you do this, you increase your vibration to that of your desire. Visualization is one of the most powerful tools for manifestation. See what you want vividly in your mind and picture as many details as you can. Try not to go into details of how, when, who, or where will it happen. This brings your energy down when you don't have those answers. Keep your focus on what you want.

- **Use affirmations to focus your mind on a high vibration.** Affirmations are positive first-person statements in the present tense with which you *affirm* what you want more of in your life. For example, when I was pregnant with my son, worst-case scenario stories and statistics continuously invaded my mind, and I was having a hard time turning them around. Affirmations did just that, though. I would repeat to myself, "My body delivers a healthy boy, all is well" anytime these lower-vibration thoughts took over. And soon, instead of going down the rabbit hole of everything bad that could happen to me and my baby, my energy was high once again. (For more on the art of affirmations, look for any of Louise Hay's books. She will always be the queen of affirmations.)

One thing that you will encounter as you work on aligning your energy with that of the Universe is that sometimes things will happen that will lower your energy. It is an inevitable part of life. After all, desire comes from things that happen, and how can desire arise if everything is perfect?

The trick is not having a perfect life but rather knowing how to align your energy to that of well-being when things are less than perfect. You need to look for the fastest way to bring your vibration back up. And here is where Step 4: Curiosity and Step 5: Compassion will help.

Pretending things are okay does not give you a high vibration. Your actions may show you are okay while your feelings and thoughts are not. You need to heal and integrate the events that lower your vibration. And that can take place only when you become curious and respond with never-ending compassion for yourself through these events.

Part of being obsessed with feeling good includes feeling your feelings, good and bad, and responding in a compassionate way that makes you feel supported and loved.

That does not mean wallowing in your feelings, as that is neither productive nor compassionate. It just means understanding that something hurt and helping yourself through the healing of that wound.

Ultimately the Law of Attraction is about strengthening our connection with ourselves and universal energy. The stuff you get to manifest into your life is just the bonus.

Advanced Manifesting: The Art of Letting Go

There is something that master manifesters know, and that is the art of letting go. What this means is letting go of control over the outcome by giving your dreams to the Universe and in turn letting it show you what it dreams for you. Control is a feeling rooted in fear, and its vibration is low. When you try to control an outcome by attempting "to make things happen," inevitably you start creating resistance toward manifestation. Of course, there is an action that is in alignment with your desire (after all, you can't win the lottery without buying a ticket), but that is a different kind of action that contributes to your desire. More on that in the next chapter, where I explain the Step of Commitment.

Letting go starts by focusing your attention on the why. The reason for this is because you can then take away your attention from all sorts of details. The when, the how, the where, and the who are not your jobs; they are the jobs of the Universe. By focusing on the why, you take your hand off the wheel and completely surrender your desire to the Universe, saying with full faith, "I know you've got this."

When you focus on the why, you also allow the Universe to surprise you. When you desire something (the what) you do so from your human perspective. This perspective is tiny compared to the gigantic perspective of the Universe. You think you know what is best for you, but only the Universe in its infinite wisdom knows the most perfect outcome for you. When you focus on the why, you are telling the Universe, "This is the vibration around this topic I seek to achieve. It is in your hands now." All you have to do then is sit back and wait as the Universe prepares something amazing with which to surprise you.

My life is bigger and richer because I have learned to step back and give the Universe permission to bring exactly what I need. I experienced this only a few years ago. At the time, I was working in the food industry, in the role I had dreamed of since the beginning of my career. I had an amazing team, I was working with great iconic brands, and doing true innovation for North America. Yet my dream job no longer seemed to fit my dream life. My son was only three years old at the time, and I was traveling constantly as my team was both in Canada and the U.S., and I was working extended hours. I was missing out on my family. Furthermore, I was asked to consider moving to the U.S. to be in the corporate office. I didn't want to leave our extended family behind. I knew something had to change.

I put my desire to the Universe, focusing on my why. I wanted to be there for my family and see my son grow up. I wanted to savor every little milestone, every new thing he learned, and I didn't want to do that through Skype. I wanted to be present. I also wanted a role where I continued to make an impact and help others while avoiding all of the travel. I also wanted to stay in Canada, my current location. After living in five countries, I was ready to finally settle down.

I then started taking inspired action, sharing my desire with close friends and sending my résumé to jobs that seemed to fill the bill and turning down those that did not. It was only a few months later, after a conversation with a friend, that a new possibility presented itself. I was talking to my friend Sarah, and she was telling me about her company. She told me her company was based in Canada and that they happened to be the second-largest employer in the country. I was curious as to who was the first one, so I asked her. "The federal government," Sarah said. I had never considered public service, but it made so much sense! It would be based in Canada! I started doing research about all of the possible jobs I could do within the government, and a few months later I found and applied to the perfect job, centered on helping companies grow through innovation. This allowed me to use my industry experience and help others achieve their dreams while helping this country I loved dearly. This was, in many ways, more perfect than I could have ever imagined.

I know for a fact that if I had continued looking for jobs in my industry, sticking to what I knew, I would have never found this amazing opportunity that far exceeded my expectations. But the Universe knew better, and it had a better plan for me. All I had to do was focus on my why and let the Universe deliver.

Letting go of control also means letting go of your need to have what you want when you want it. It is about trusting the perfect timing of the Universe. It knows the right time in your life for you to receive what you want.

If something has not yet manifested, it could be because you are not ready to receive it yet. For example, you may be looking for a partner, but the Law of Attraction works by attracting people of similar vibrations. So if your partner has not shown up yet, it may just mean the Universe is doing you a favor by not bringing someone that matches your vibration at that time, as your vibration is out of whack and someone with a similar vibration would just be a total disaster. In this case, the best use of your energy is focusing on becoming the person you want to attract, so that you know the Universe will bring you the most perfect person.

It could also mean your order is not ready yet. If you picture the Law of Attraction as you placing an order at a restaurant, it takes time to create the perfect dish. Sit back, relax, and know your desire is on its way.

Know that letting go of control may also mean that some events or circumstances you don't expect may show up in your life. These events may be something you sometimes classify as "wrong." But it's important to remember that the Universe is always working in your favor, and what may seem less than ideal may just be a way for the Universe to help you get closer to what you want.

For example, you may have in your vibration the desire to change to a new position at work. You keep your energy high, you focus on your why, and then you lose your current job. I know this would seem very scary, and you may need to take some time to grieve and regain your ground after an event such as this. Keep your faith that something is in the works. It may just mean that you had to let go of your current job before a new one could manifest into your experience.

Keep the faith. Like author Byron Katie says: "Everything happens for you, not to you." Take your hand off the wheel and let the Universe do the driving.

Recognize the Signs Around You

Another thing to keep in mind when manifesting is that as your desire starts to get closer to your experience, you will start seeing signs. If you are looking to manifest a car, you may suddenly see cars like the one you have been thinking about everywhere you go. Or someone may approach you and say, "You know, my office is looking for someone just like you," even though you never mentioned to this person that you were looking for a new job. Watch for signs. They are a great way to receive confirmation from the Universe that what you want is on its way.

Sometimes, however, you may misread the signs. You may see something and think, *This is it! This is my manifestation*, and when things don't happen as you expect, you get deflated and take it as evidence that the Law doesn't work, when in reality it's a sign that your manifestation is around the corner. For example, this happens sometimes when looking for a job. You may be taking lots of positive action by sending résumés, sharing your plans with friends, and all of a sudden the most amazing, perfect job shows up for you, and you think, *This is it! This is my job!* You interview and you ace it. Soon you start planning your outfit for your first day at the office and even what you will bring for lunch that day. And then, you don't get a call back.

At this point you may think, *The Law doesn't work* or *There is something wrong with me.* You ignore the fact that that near miss with an amazing job was a sign that something even more perfect for you is coming your way, and because you already let lower-vibration thoughts take over, you start slowing down all the great well-being that is on its way to you. If this happens, take a step back and look at things from a different perspective. Give yourself a chance to believe that everything is working out for your highest good. Because it is.

Signs also show up when you are attracting into your life something you don't want. If you don't want to get sick, for example, you may start seeing people around you calling in sick, or your neighbor all of a sudden tells you there was a big outbreak of an illness at school. Take this as your sign to turn your focus from sickness to health.

Author James Redfield says, "Where attention goes, energy flows." This is a great opportunity to look at the signs and readjust where you are focusing your attention if it is not on something you want. You get to decide what gets activated into your vibration, and you get to bring it into your experience through alignment.

At the end of the day, these steps boil down to simple advice: Become obsessed with feeling good. The Universe will take care of the rest. It is the Law.

¿Y Cómo?

The Cloning Exercise

The objective of this exercise is to create the feelings that you will feel once your why is delivered; you want to create the exact vibration that will attract your desire into form.

Start by finding a time when you will not be interrupted and a place where you can be by yourself. Decide at the beginning of this exercise that you will be honest, and allow yourself to experience the feelings of your wish having manifested, even if you do not yet know the details of how that will happen. Have pen and paper ready.

Begin by reading your work in the Why Exercise from the previous chapter, where you articulated in detail the why of what you want. After you reread the exercise, focus on the feeling that you will have when that why is delivered to you. Close your eyes and visualize for a few minutes that why being delivered to you. Enjoy the feeling of your wish being manifested. Once you have completely experienced what it would feel like to have that desire come into your experience, write it down. Describe the feeling in as much detail as possible.

Once you have finished writing about your feeling, brainstorm three ways you can "clone" that feeling right now. Come up with at least three activities you could do now that would give you a similar feeling.

For example, perhaps you want a bigger house and your why is so each member of your household can have a space they can call their own and you can have a beautiful space to entertain friends. When that why is delivered, you will feel your home is spacious and beautiful. You will feel called to share this beautiful space with others and create beautiful memories.

To achieve that same feeling of spaciousness, you could declutter your current space. You could also update your decor slightly to give you the same feeling of pride in having a beautiful space you can share. You could start to invite friends over to create beautiful memories in your current space as you wait for the new one. Doing these things will clone the feeling of a new and better house, so you can achieve the correct vibration to manifest your desire of a new home.

The Filtering-Out Exercise

The objective of this exercise is to identify activities and people in your life who are negatively impacting your ability to maintain a high vibration. I do not believe that other people transfer their energy to us, but I do believe that at times we use things and people we observe as an excuse to lower our vibration. As we begin to be more mindful of our energy, we can start filtering out and removing from our life these situations and people, whenever possible.

As you become better at understanding your triggers using the techniques described in Step 4: Curiosity and Step 5: Compassion, you may no longer need this exercise as much. However, over time it will continue to be a great way to reset your energy and take a break when the overall experience of dealing with undesirable things in your life becomes a bit overwhelming.

Start by finding a time when you will not be interrupted and a place where you can be by yourself. Decide at the beginning of this exercise that you will be honest about the things, situations, and people in your life that no longer contribute to your highest good. Allow yourself the space to be sincere.

Close your eyes, take a deep breath, and start going through a day in your life. Identify the things, people, and situations that cause you stress, anxiety, sadness, or any kind of feeling that takes away your peace. Notice if that feeling is consistent every time you come in contact with the things you've identified.

Then open your eyes. Now consider whether there is a way to experience these things, people, or situations a little less in your life. For example, you may find, like I did, that watching the news makes you feel stressed and sad. If that is the case, you could decide that you will limit or no longer watch the news. You might also notice that a certain person seems to constantly drag you into their chismes and their drama. You may decide to take a break from that person. Another situation may be that a certain food group or snack makes you feel heavy or depressed after eating it, in which case you may decide that it is best to avoid it as much as possible.

As you implement this exercise, you may notice things becoming easier in your day-to-day life, which is a great indication that you were using these things, people, and events as an excuse to lower your energy. If you would like to better understand the reasons behind it, you can do so in Step 4: Curiosity, and you may come up with ways to support yourself in Step 5: Compassion.

As you implement these steps, your energy will be less dependent on external circumstances. Your vibration will naturally stay at the level of well-being that is your natural set point.

The Juicing Exercise

The objective of this exercise is to really allow yourself to enjoy the feeling of your wish becoming your experience. I love the term *juicing* because of the visual of taking a fruit and extracting its sweet nectar. In this exercise you will take a fantastic dream and extract the sweetness you will experience when you achieve it. As you do this, your energy will reach a high vibration that will become a great point of attraction for your desire. If you would like to access this exercise as a pre-recorded guided meditation, you can find it at www.sandrahinojosaludwig.com /chicawhynot.

Start by finding a time when you will not be interrupted and a place where you can be by yourself. Decide at the beginning of this exercise that you will allow yourself to enjoy visualizing your wish in the present time, even if you don't yet know when, how, or where it will come or who may bring it to you. Don't doubt your ability to manifest this desire, and instead just focus on it.

Sit in a comfortable position. Take a deep breath and close your eyes. Breathe in and out. Start visualizing your wish in the present. You are in the middle of enjoying the amazing creation in front of you. Look at everything around you—your clothes, your hair, and the objects in your midst. Feel the temperature of the room on your arms or the breeze if you are outside. Now look around at your magnificent creation. Make it as real as you can.

Now that you can clearly see your manifestation, let it move into your heart. Put your hand over your heart and breathe deeply into the feeling.

Identify the feeling of seeing this wish, and let yourself feel gratitude to the Universe for providing and to yourself for having this desire. Feel the joy and the greatness that exist within you. The promise of creation lives within you, and the feeling is that of oneness with the stream of well-being of the Universe. Feel the desire to laugh and cry. Feel the desire to drop to your knees and say thank you.

Experience how the words *thank you* are not big enough for the feeling you wish to convey. Your biggest desire is now here, it's yours, and your happiness and peace mingle in your heart in a sweet dance. Feel the sweetness of the moment and the vastness of the Universe within you.

Move your body slightly in a sweet celebration for everything the Universe has provided to you. Whisper "thank you." Now breathe deeply. Stay in this space for as long as you can.

As you open your eyes, thank the Universe one more time. Your wish is on its way.

Sí, Pero

- **"How can I be positive if this person is always chingándome (bothering me)?"** If there is a person who is always bothering you, there are two actions you can take. First, you could filter them out of your life permanently or for a while as you work on your triggers around this person. The second action you could take is to try to identify the reasons why their actions bother you so much. They may be doing things that offend you or make you feel attacked. They may in fact be attacking you. Use Step 4: Curiosity to understand why their actions are such a trigger in your life. Once you understand the beliefs that this person activates in you, use Step 5: Compassion to set the right boundaries and take the right actions that will make these situations easier on you. This may mean letting them go from your life. If this person happens to be a close relation such as your mom, your dad, your sibling, or your husband, know that love is accepting them as they are, instead of wanting to change them, and that healthy boundaries may even improve the relationship. If you are unable to enact boundaries, know that it is possible to continue to love people even in the absence of communication. Keeping someone who is negative or destructive in your life is not a requirement. No es manda (It is not a promise to the Virgin).

- **"How can I be positive when something really bad has happened in my life?"** Bad things will happen; it's part of life. In fact, it's part of the process of creation, as your desire can only grow from situations that are not what you would like them to be. If what has happened to you is something big, like the loss of a loved one, an unfortunate medical diagnosis, or the loss of something dear to you like your home or your job, be compassionate and allow yourself the time to grieve that loss. Use Step 5: Compassion in this book to help navigate through the grief. Little by little, as you allow yourself to feel the pain, you will slowly start to regain the ground beneath your feet. As you do this, gently start considering ways to slowly raise your vibration. If the sadness that you experience is consistent and does not decrease in intensity over time, consider consulting a therapist to help you cope with your feelings.

- **"I did everything in the book, and I didn't get what I wanted. What did I do wrong?"** There are a few reasons why manifestation may not have occurred for you yet. First, verify that you have clarity on what you want and that your desire is integral, authentic, positive, and specific as described in Step 1: Clarity. Then look at the intention behind your energy. If your intention is to control the when, the where, the who, and the how, maybe you are in a situation where you need to practice surrender. Surrender can be a scary thing, especially if you come from a place where you have had to be self-sufficient your whole life. Know that surrendering is entrusting your dream to the Universe, which is the overall source of well-being. If letting go of control seems too scary, start with small things where you let go and surrender to the Universe, like the color of the next shirt you buy or the flavor of your birthday cake. As you strengthen your trust in the Universe "muscle" and gain confidence in your ability as a manifester, letting go and surrendering may get easier. It could also be the case that you are not seeing results because the Universe has a specific plan for you with its own perfect timing. Be patient. Remember the quote from *A Course in Miracles*: "Infinite patience delivers immediate results."

- **"I think what I want is just too big and I doubt it will happen."** Trust that if you are given a dream, it's because the Universe has those plans for you and intends to help you achieve them. Anything that comes into your dreams is possible if you allow each dream to thrive and come into your life. Focus on your why, as this will help remove resistance from your manifestation while giving the Universe the space to surprise you in ways you never thought possible.

- **"I would like to manifest something in the life of someone else."** As you have seen in this chapter, the Universe responds to your own energy. Because of this, it is not possible to manifest in someone else's life. I understand that at times it may be painful to see a loved one who is unable to bring into their life what they want, but what manifests in someone else's life is purely the result of their own vibration as it relates to that topic. If you want to help that person, make yourself available to them in case they wish to talk about your experience of manifesting, but do so without expectations. Know that you can't force them to live the Law of Attraction and that unsolicited advice may, in fact, not be something they would appreciate at the moment. Maybe the best thing you can do for them is to be present when they are looking for someone to be with them as they deal with something undesirable while living your best life as a manifester. The best way to guide a boat to shore is by being a lighthouse shining its light so others can find the shore.

- **"Something I didn't ask for manifested into my experience. How is that possible?"** As I've shared in this chapter, many times the step of asking is done unconsciously when we notice something could be different and believe that different would be better. If your energy happens to be a match to that desire, you have then manifested something you didn't know you wished for. If the event you manifested is something undesirable, know that regardless of what has manifested, the Universe is always working in your favor. Trust that something good will come out of it in your experience. As author Gabby Bernstein would say, trust that "the Universe has your back."

Chapter 4

Step 3:
COMMITMENT

Step by Step

"Congratulations! On behalf of the Vancouver 2010 Olympic Torch Relay, we're pleased to confirm that you are one of the Olympic torchbearers who will soon hold history in your hand when you carry the Olympic flame in the Vancouver 2010 Torch Relay."

I looked at the e-mail in front of me with my mouth open, stunned. I had heard about moments that take your breath away, and this was one of them. I soon brought my hand to my mouth as if to remind it to close. My brain was frozen for a second, as I didn't know how to process the words in the e-mail.

Then it hit me. I had been chosen. I screamed in joy.

This was the culmination of months of work, getting myself closer and closer to this day, one step at a time. And now I was going to be an Olympic torchbearer, like the ones I saw on my television back home in Monterrey. My mom would tell me, "Apúrate, mija" ("Hurry up, daughter"), calling me to the living room whenever they would light the Olympic flame in Greece. My mom has always loved all things Greek, and the Olympic flame ceremony was no different. I watched on TV as the women in white flowy dresses held the flame ceremoniously and then gave it to the torchbearers. This was the start of a journey of thousands of miles toward the final destination: the Olympic stadium of the host country for that year's games.

And now I got to carry it too. It was, in a way, a tribute to Olympians who I admired so much. It was my own way of wearing the Olympic rings. And honoring the chica in me who saw herself in people going after their dreams.

Let me back up a bit.

As a girl I was never into sports, in part because I always came in last in any track and field event, but more than anything because I just preferred dancing, singing, and theater.

My mom says that even as a little girl I was always a performer, singing in front of my audience, which usually consisted of my abuelitos, my parents, and whichever sibling I could rope in against their will to see me perform. My neighbors and I would choreograph dances to Timbiriche and Parchís on front porches and sometimes in the middle of the street.

In elementary school, I took it one step further, signing up for everything from choir to traditional Mexican dancing to theater. I loved the feeling of being in front of an audience, making them laugh, cry, and gasp. I loved transforming myself into whoever I was to play that day, stepping into their shoes and their world.

I also loved my theater teacher. She worked on a local TV channel and performed in a professional theater. I admired her and wanted to be her, if only to feel what it was like to be an actress. She introduced me to the art of surrendering to a role and falling in love with my voice.

Everything about performing made my heart sing, and I was also good at it. I even won nominations and awards for best actress in my state.

Yet, sometime after grade six, my dream started slowly fading away. Academics replaced my love of performing, in part because being an actress just didn't seem like a respectable career to my family. Like a good Mexican girl, I followed my family's wishes for my life into a respectable degree in engineering followed by a master's in science. After all, nothing says respectable like math and science.

During grad school in the U.S., I joined a graduate association that raises funds by doing catering. It was a great way to meet people. It was also a great way to earn cash, as all the money earned by the association was divided among its members at the end of the semester. As a poor graduate student, there was no better deal, as you could get as much at $500 for a semester's work. That usually paid for my ticket home for Christmas.

One of the events we covered during my tenure as a starving student/caterer was a volleyball game in which the U.S. Olympic team was playing. After the game we got to serve them, and we saw athlete after athlete come and get their food from our station, exhausted from their game, yet with a smile that I recognized from my performing days. It was the smile of doing what you loved, of doing what made your heart sing.

They reminded me of the part of myself that was buried under calculus formulas and chemistry reactions.

I wanted to learn more about the athletes and what had driven them to live their dream. They all had Olympic ring tattoos, and I asked one of them to tell me more about his. He told me about attending the Olympics and the work he put into everything he did, and the satisfaction of being one of the few in the world who got to say, "I went to the Olympics."

Years later, when working, I also got to meet Olympic curling athletes whom my company sponsored. I heard them speak about their dedication and their ability to let go of anything that didn't help them reach their dream. They had faith in the fact that every step they took got them closer to their dream. Their resilience, strength, love, and hope were inspiring.

Those two encounters made me fascinated with the Olympics and its athletes. It was enthralling to hear their stories of triumph and loss and to learn about their unseen preparation, work, and hardship. The innate talent and the determination that went with it was amazing. And it all boiled down to one moment every four years.

To me, the Olympics represented doing what you love, what makes your heart sing, working for it with unwavering hope, and baring your soul for all of the world to see, just like performing.

Years later, when the company that I was working for announced that it was sponsoring the Olympics in Vancouver and that it had been allocated a torchbearer placement that would be raffled off among employees, I knew I had to win it. Wearing the rings felt like a way to honor the girl in me who loved to bare her soul and was fascinated by determination and hope.

It was no ordinary raffle, though. You couldn't just buy tickets. You had to earn the ballots by going the extra mile at work and having colleagues recognize that extra work by nominating you for the torchbearer spot. Each nomination meant a ballot with your name on it. At the end, the president of the company was going to stand in front of everyone and pick one name, the name of the person who would get to wear the Olympic rings.

I knew I had to do my best. And so I flew into action. I tried to be helpful to all my colleagues in the hope that I would get more and more nominations. I did everything from gathering data for other people's trials in the plant to doing research for other colleagues to covering the desk in reception a couple of times. I believed helping others would get me closer to my goal, so I kept going. I didn't know exactly what else to do, but when inspiration showed me a new way, I followed without question. I was determined. And I canvased like I was running for president. I knew that even though the raffle was out of my control, my ability to influence nominations was not. I worked hard to do everything that was within my power.

By then I knew about the Law of Attraction, so I also made every effort possible to keep my energy high. I stopped taking part in any activities that didn't serve my energy, such as watching the news and arguing with people. Instead, I filled my life with activities that made me happy, such as dancing and spending time with loved ones. I was in the groove. I visualized myself carrying the torch and the feelings that came with it.

When the day of the raffle came, I was convinced my name would be the one called. I stood at the front so I could easily go and get my prize. I was even practicing in my mind the humble thank-you I would say when my name was called. I was ecstatic.

Then the name was called . . . and it was not mine. I didn't get it. I was crestfallen.

I didn't know what had gone wrong. I took all the actions and did all the alignment! I went home, feeling a bit down, thinking all my work hadn't helped me achieve what I wanted. I was puzzled as to why the Law of Attraction hadn't worked for me.

I conveyed my loss to my boyfriend, Finnegan. He listened to my sad story and then very calmly said, "Sorry you lost. You know there are a lot of other contests you could apply to, right?" I felt new hope. "There are?" I said. Finnegan's voice that day sounded very much like the voice of inspiration, like the Universe whispering new ways I could continue pursuing my dream.

I didn't know it back then, but the raffle was just a sign. I was getting closer to my dream, and even if my name was not called, the fact that I could participate was a sign that I was on my way. As I shared in Step 2: Collaboration, the Universe sends you signs when you are getting closer. And the raffle was my sign.

With my newfound inspiration, I went into action. My goal remained unchanged, but I shifted my strategy to match the new circumstances. I immediately researched and found three large companies that had promotions where clients could apply for a chance to carry the Olympic torch. They all asked for entry forms to be filled out. Within days I had filled and submitted all the forms.

Weeks later, I got an e-mail from a soft drink company asking me to provide more information. I did. Then weeks after that, I received another e-mail asking me to write an essay about how I looked after the environment. I didn't write the essay.

¿¿¿Queeeé??? (Whaaaat????)

¡Ya sé! (I know!)

I missed the deadline. But as is usually the case, the Universe was already moving with great speed to grant me my wish, and it was literally reorganizing everything to help me manifest it. The day after I realized I had missed the deadline, I got an e-mail saying that the deadline had been extended!

Not wanting to tempt faith, I got to work and completed the assignment that same day. A few weeks later, I got a message asking me for a police background check. I took care of that. And then, a few weeks after that, I got an e-mail saying: "Congratulations! You are one of the Olympic torchbearers." The e-mail contained details about where I would carry the torch and asked for information regarding the size for my uniform.

It was official. I would wear the rings!

I didn't even know these contests existed when I first tried to become a torchbearer. I now know I didn't need to. With each step came additional inspiration from the Universe and a new perspective that made finding the next step easier. Above all, I had plenty of confidence that things would work out as long as I did my part. All I had to do was listen to inspiration and put one foot in front of the other, step by step, letting the path appear before me.

Inspired Action

Previously I talked about how energy creates the things and situations that we experience every day. I explained that in order to manifest our desires, we must align our energy.

Here is the thing: There is NO bigger energy in the Universe than action. The Universe listens to action and says, "I see you are serious; let's do this!"

After all, you can't win the lottery if you don't buy a ticket. It takes inspired action.

The first time I heard the term *inspired action* was from Rhonda Byrne in *The Secret*, my introduction to the Law of Attraction. It wasn't long after that I also heard it from Abraham Hicks, and later from other teachers of the Law.

Inspiration is "a sudden good idea," according to the *Cambridge Dictionary*. Inspiration comes from the Latin *inspirare*, meaning "into breath" or "breathe into." Inspiration is the ideas that the Universe breathes into you.

Inspired action is different from ordinary action in that it is aligned with your bigger desire and with the universal energy. When you take inspired action, you may still feel fear or hesitation, but in your mind it is a simple decision to take that action. It feels like the natural next best step. And although it can feel daunting, you know you can do it. It feels within reach, either because you have all the resources needed or because the Universe is providing you with inspiration along the way.

Inspiration can come in the way of comments from others, through advertising, through your favorite TV show, a newspaper article, or meeting someone who has followed it before. It can also come through dreams or ideas that appear in your mind suddenly. Once inspiration comes, the next step becomes clear and feels manageable.

Inspired action is not one of control, which would be based on fear, but one of joy, which means it is in full alignment with the Universe that creates worlds. Inspired action also brings with it peace, as you move forward with the certainty that there is nothing more you could have done to bring your desire to you.

For manifestation to exist, both alignment and inspired action need to exist. Alignment without inspired action is wishful thinking and feels like begging for a hero to come and save you. Action without alignment is based in fear and feels like trying to control a situation. Alignment combined with inspired action creates miracles and feels like surrender combined with full conviction that the Universe's highest good for you is on its way.

Author Joseph Campbell once said, "I have found that you have only to take that one step toward the gods, and they will then take ten steps toward you." Begin. Take that next best step toward the gods.

Where to Find Inspiration

Now, as we all know, the path doesn't always seem clear; in fact, sometimes it's hard to see it at all. Fear not: Inspiration is something you can attract into your life.

Here are some things to consider if the path seems a bit blurry:

- **Be open to receive.** At times you may still find it hard to decide what the first step is going to be. In this case, your first step is to open your eyes and ears to inspiration; that act alone will help you get there.

- **Look around you for inspiration.** You can start by sharing the idea you have with close friends whom you trust. Their comments and feedback could be valuable in finding the next step, just like my friend Sarah helped me take the next step toward the perfect job I never knew I wanted.

- **Look for role models.** Find people who have walked the path before you. One truth is that everything in the world has been done. Want to be a telenovela star? Already done! Want to be a millionaire? Already done! Want to be a mom? Already done! Want to raise a Xoloitzcuintli (Mexican hairless dog)? Already done!

Author Helene Hegemann said, "There's no such thing as originality, just authenticity." What this means is that all ideas already exist. What is unique is your own special way of expressing and executing them. As such, someone out there has done what you want to do. Find them. With the Internet at the tip of your fingers, you can look on LinkedIn, read biographies, and join groups of common interests on Facebook. Find inspiration in the steps that people took before you. Then as you set foot on your path, inject your own authenticity into your journey as the Universe inevitably starts whispering in your ear what is the next best step for you.

I remember once listening to the story of José M. Hernández, a former NASA astronaut and the son of Mexican immigrants living in California. After watching the Apollo 17 mission on TV in 1972, a 10-year-old José set his goal to become an astronaut. He went to university to prepare for his dream. He applied to NASA for the first time at 30 years old, and he got rejected. He kept applying only to be rejected a total of 11 times. After about six rejections, he realized there was something he was missing from his plan. He looked at all the people who had been selected and realized they all were pilots. That was his next best step. He became a pilot. At age 42, he finally realized his dream of becoming an astronaut. Four years later, he made it to space. Imitation is said to be a form of flattery, but it is also a smart move that helps point the way. Why reinvent the wheel when there are so many examples out there?

- **Find a community.** Surround yourself with a team of people who will see your vision for your future and cheer you along the way. Something that also struck me about José's stories is that he shared his dream of becoming an astronaut early on with his dad. His dad said to him, "I think you can do it."

  If you know your desire is authentic and integral, as described in Step 1: Clarity, know that there will be people out there who will see that and, no matter how big a dream it is, will support you and cheer you along the way. Know also that some people may not support you, and that's okay. Sometimes people may project their own fears onto your desire. After all, dreaming big feels vulnerable for many of us. Look for the people in your life who will tell you, "I think you can do it." Sometimes having that wind behind you can make all the difference.

- **Understand your limitations.** There may be a time when on the path toward what you want you may realize you lack some skills to get to where you want to go. That's expected if you're going after something outside your comfort zone. Look for the experts. After all, sometimes it's not *what* you know, it's *who* you know and what *they* know. There will always be someone who will hold the key to exactly the door you wish to open. In this case, that is your next best step—finding that expert. Do your research and find people who may know the domain. Eventually someone will point the way.

- **Listen to inspiration.** Many times you may decide to listen to your intuition. However, when you do that, you may be relying only on your human nature. *Intuition*, according to the *Cambridge Dictionary*, is the ability to understand or know something immediately based on your feelings rather than facts. When you focus on inspiration, you allow yourself to connect to Spirit and its guidance. Inspiration will feel like common logic even in the absence of evidence. It will feel like there is no other thing you should be doing differently, and it will feel good. And although you may experience nervousness over the step it suggests, you know it is the right next best step. Inspiration connects with you in the silence. If you are having trouble connecting to it, remove the noise from your life, even if just for one minute, by making the intentional decision to allow yourself some time in silence, just being and breathing. Inspiration may not readily talk to you during these quiet moments, but as you do this more and more, it will be like sending an invitation for it to come into your life, and it may actually manifest even in your busiest day.

- **Jump.** You may also find that you know the first few steps, but you don't have visibility to see all of them. As Martin Luther King Jr. said, "Take the first step in faith. You don't have to see the whole staircase, just take the first step." We may think that for us to get to our destination, the whole path needs to be known. But the truth is that many times, especially when you are going after something that is big in your life and outside your comfort zone, the path will only appear once you start walking. So even if you don't know what comes next, trust that the path will reveal itself. Because it will. This is how I went after my graduate studies, as I described in Chapter 1, even though I was offered funding only for the first year. Inspiration spoke to me through my friend telling me not to worry. And I never had to, just as the Universe had promised.

- **Become curious.** At times you may also feel like you know the next step but feel paralyzed to take it. Or you find yourself unable to make a decision about which step to take next. Some steps, after all, may feel very transformative for your life, and taking those steps may mean leaving behind your life as you know it, such as moving to a new city, leaving a relationship, or switching careers. If the step is clear but the fear is too big, become curious about what is behind that fear. Try to identify the things that fear is telling you are scary. The next chapter will be invaluable in helping bring light to those dark areas inside of you that insist on telling you stories of gloom and doom.

- **Trust the perfection.** Like my wise teacher Abraham Hicks would say, "You can never get it wrong, because it is never done." Even if you take a step that seems to take you on a different path from what you had initially intended, trust that it was the perfect step for you to take. The new perspective you have gained has only added clarity to your desire, and the Universe will respond in kind by showing you a new, different way. At any time you can reframe your plan and once again take the next best step.

- **Adjust your strategy.** You may also find that external situations demand you approach your plan in a different way, just as happened to me when I didn't win my company's spot for the torchbearer position. When that happens, what is important is not what happened to you, but how you respond to it. Resilience is the capacity to recover quickly from difficulties, and it is a skill you can acquire. Become resilient by accepting what is and gently changing your strategy to something that feels good and authentic to you and your why while getting you closer to what you want. If needed, grieve the loss of the path you thought would get you there and accept the new path you must follow. When you're ready, dust yourself off and take the next best step from your newly found perspective while keeping your goal in mind.

  This works even if the situation that occurred is life changing. Here, focusing on your why, as explained in the previous chapter, is so important, because it will open you to new ways to reach for your why in this new chapter of your life. Even if the wind changes, you can always adjust your sail to get to your destination. As pastor and author Charles Swindoll says, "Life is 10 percent what happens to you and 90 percent how you react to it."

- **Make perseverance, not perfection, your superpower.** If you have ever been to a dance cardio class, you know that they tell you not to give up but continue moving at your own pace if you lose your breath or find it too challenging. You may feel like running as far away from the room to the beat of any Daddy Yankee song, but resist the temptation. And commit. Every morning ask yourself, *What step can I take today to get me closer to what I want?* Keep on moving.

  Things will happen and steps you thought were the ones to get you closer may not turn out as you want. Keep moving. What may be perceived as a failure may just be a lesson from the Universe telling you "it is not that way." Persevere until your inspiration tells you otherwise.

- **Be patient.** At times you may take action and see little change. You work and work and see little to show for it. Consider that maybe you are not taking inspired action but rather actions rooted in your desire to control. If that is the case, take a step back and try to connect with your inspiration for guidance, following the exercises at the end of this chapter. Also, remember that Rome was not build in a day, and it may take time to see results. As Bill Gates famously said, "Most people overestimate what they can do in one year and underestimate what they can do in ten years." Continue putting one foot in front of the other, trusting that every little action is getting you closer to what you want.

As the path becomes clearer, your confidence will sky-rocket. With each step you will feel your desire starting to manifest. You will feel the joy of collaborating with the Universe to create your desire.

Soon you will feel full of goals and dreams, and when so many things are possible it may actually become a bit overwhelming to decide what the next step should be. Don't worry.

As you saw in the previous chapter, the process of aligning your energy is the same for anything you desire in your life. Furthermore, things in your life do not happen in isolation. As such, there is no need to overwhelm yourself with all the work that you believe is necessary to reach all of your goals.

Take inspired action in only one or two goals. As you start to pursue those desires, the Universe will rearrange itself and start bringing you closer to things that you are not even working on yet. Trust your inspiration.

Remember that no dream is given to you without the ability to reach it. The Universe has in fact put this dream in your heart. It is its best effort to call you to be the person you were meant to be, to show you the plans it has for you. The Universe, after all, is the biggest dreamer. Walk unafraid and determined to go for it. The ability to reach for it is within you. The Universe is pushing you forward every step of the way. Let inspiration help. And take the next best step.

¿Y Cómo?

The Brainstorming Exercise

The objective of this exercise is to come up with ideas for what may be the next best step for you. This exercise can be done alone, but you may benefit from doing some prework by chatting with your team before you do the exercise. Remember that your team is made of friends who can see your vision for your future and are there with you, cheering you on every step of the way.

If you wish to do the prework of the exercise, start by selecting a group of three to five friends. Meet them one by one, either for a walk or a coffee or a long chat on Zoom or WhatsApp or another platform. Meet in a place where you can connect and talk uninterrupted. Prior to asking for their advice, reiterate that you are committed to your dream and you are looking for advice on next steps, not for opinions about whether the goal you have for yourself is the best goal for you at this time. Share your dream with them and ask for advice about the steps they think could be your next best steps. You're looking for steps, not inspiration, since someone else's inspiration can never be your own compass. Take notes. After all, más vale una tinta pálida que una mente brillante (a pale ink is better than a bright mind). Repeat these interviews with all of your selected friends. Then start the exercise.

For this exercise, start by finding a time when you will not be interrupted and a place where you can be by yourself. Decide at the beginning of this exercise that you will be honest and allow yourself to trust in your inspiration.

On a piece of paper, write all the steps that come to mind that could get you closer to your goal. Don't worry about sequence, or the how, when, where, or who. Just write everything and anything that comes to mind. If you did the prework, include in this list all the steps that you learned from your meetings. Once you are finished, look at the list and every step on it. Listen for inspiration. Do any of the steps call your name?

Separate the ideas into three categories: Not Now, Maybe, and For Sure using the table below. You can download the template for this exercise at www.sandrahinojosaludwig.com/chicawhynot.

Not Now	Maybe	For Sure

Once you're finished, leave the exercise alone for the day. In a day or two, review the list again and notice if any new inspirations have arrived since you last saw it. Write down whatever you feel is not yet on the list.

If in between writing and revisiting the list you get an idea, write it down or type it into your phone. Do not let these wonderful inspiration downloads be forgotten.

Here is an example of a list I could have built when I had the goal to become a torchbearer:

Not Now	Maybe	For Sure
• Find out which community groups will be selecting torchbearers • Join community groups that will be selecting torchbearers	• Apply to all torchbearer contests in Canada • Organize the next team event • Offer to do a training for operators • Say no when colleague who makes me feel bad invites me out	Ways to get more votes/nominations: • Tell colleagues about my desire; ask for advice on how to get their nomination (at least one colleague per dept) • Help in reception • Offer to help colleague with trial • Do a search of all torchbearer contests in Canada • Feel good every day! (Law of Attraction) • Stop watching news • Stop complaining at work—constructive suggestions only

Now commit. Commit to taking at least one step from the For Sure list. If the activity is too big, break it down into smaller pieces. For example, if you wrote "buy a car," the next best step may be to look at your finances to determine the price of a car you can afford, or how much you need to save for one. Remember, you are not striving for perfection; what you are going for is action. Just take a step. The next best step. Keep moving as if you were cardio dancing to your favorite song. If you find it terrifying to take a step or you find it difficult to decide what to do, go read the next chapter about Curiosity, and try to shed some light on the fears that are stopping you.

The Benchmarking Exercise

The objective of this exercise is to identify actions that you could take based on people who have walked your intended path before you.

Start by finding a time when you will not be interrupted and a place where you can be by yourself. Decide at the beginning of this exercise that you will persevere toward finding the best information and you will be honest about your abilities when compared to what is required. Allow yourself the space to be sincere.

Now research and identify people who have accomplished what you wish to accomplish.

For example, if you wish to get a job as a marketing analyst, type "marketing analyst" into LinkedIn and find people who do that job. Look at what they did to get there: their education, their experience, and their skills. Create a composite of what it takes to be a marketing analyst by looking at a number of them. Also look at current job postings. Identify the requirements being sought in potential candidates.

If your desire is to achieve a goal like becoming an Olympic soccer player, read the Wikipedia pages for soccer superstars like Abby Wambach or Megan Rapinoe. Listen to their interviews. Try to identify the steps they took to become Olympic soccer players. Based on what you read, research the schools they mention, or the programs they were in, or the teams they joined. Make a composite of what it takes to become an Olympic soccer player from what you learned through your research.

Now that you have a composite, list it in the Requirements list below. You can download the template for this exercise at www.sandrahinojosaludwig .com/chicawhynot.

Requirements	My Level vs. Requirements	Possible Steps

Next, on the list labeled "My Level vs. Requirements" rate yourself in relation to the requirements, and be very honest. What skills, abilities, or education are you missing? Now fill in the next steps you could take to close the gap between where you are (My Level) versus where you want to be (Requirements).

Here is an example of a list I could have created when I had the goal to attend graduate school in the U.S. for food science:

Requirements	My Level vs. Requirements	Possible Steps

• GPA of 3.0 or higher
• English proficiency
• Acceptable GRE
• Science-based classes
• Good recommendations
• $5k savings per semester for living, $5k for tuition (unless research assistantship for in-state tuition—$3k and salary)
• Student visa
	• GPA is 3.4
	• English proficiency unknown
	• Acceptable GRE: unsure
	• Science-based classes: done
	• Good recommendations
	• Currently have $2.5k saved total
	• No visa yet
		• English: Take TOEFL
		  • Schedule, pay, take it
		• Acceptable GRE
		  • Prepare, schedule, pay, take it
		• Get 3 recommendation letters (need only 2)
		• Save $2.5k more
		• Contact professors for research assistantships (in selected schools)
		• When acceptance letter received, apply

Now commit. Commit to taking at least one step from the "Possible Steps" list. If the activity is too big, break it down into smaller pieces. For example, if you wrote "open a restaurant," the next best step may be to research what permits you will need or to make a budget of the initial investment needed and general operating costs.

Remember, you're not going for perfection; what you are going for is action. Just take a step. The next best step. And keep moving. If you find it terrifying to take a step or you find it difficult to decide what to do, go to the next chapter about Curiosity, and try to shed some light on the fears that are stopping you.

Sí, Pero

- **"I don't know all the steps I need to take to achieve my goal."** It will take faith to go after what you want. Even if you knew all the steps from point A, where you are, to point B, where you want to be, life could always throw you curveballs, or things may not be exactly as you had first assumed. It's okay; learn to be fluid, just like a river that is trying to reach the sea. If you are a planner like me, it may feel yucky to go ahead without a solid plan. Don't let your need to be in control take over. Remember, control is rooted in fear and is a feeling of low vibration.

  I remember when I first took a role as a group leader at my last company. It was such a rush, as it was my dream job from the beginning of my career. I led a team of 13 scientists and soon learned that there were many things I couldn't control. It felt overwhelming, as there were many moving pieces and many more that were out of my control. It was then that I reached out to Jonathan, a colleague of mine who had been doing a similar job for a long time. I asked him how he dealt with the craziness, and he told me in a very calm and relaxed way, "What can I tell you, Sandra, I am comfortable being uncomfortable." Like Jonathan suggested to me that day, the answer is never to try and control everything so you feel comfortable, but to learn to be uncomfortable in the uncertainty and chaos. And go with the flow.

- **"I don't have all the resources to do all or some of the steps."** If this is the case, maybe your next best step is to acquire those resources, whether they are new skills or financing. Do what is within your reach at this time. As you will learn in the next chapter, *excuse* is another word for fear. Remember not to look for perfection but perseverance. Adjust as needed and keep moving forward.

- **"External circumstances outside my control prevent me from reaching my goal."** There will be times when the exact goal you would like to see may seem a bit out of reach. For example, if you are in your 40s and would like to be an Olympic gymnast but can't even turn a cartwheel, take a step back as described in Chapter 2, and identify your why. You may find that the reason behind your desire is that you want to have a strong body, or because you want to put the name of your country on the podium, or because you want to be recognized as the best at something so you can be a role model to other Latinas, or simply because you love the sport. Try to look for ways to deliver those whys into your life in ways other than your original idea of becoming an Olympic athlete. You may decide that you will pursue a strong body by lifting weights, or you could become a volunteer to help athletes make it to the podium, or you could write a blog about the sport. Remember what it is that you love that makes you want to pursue that goal, and let that love be your guide to the next best step.

- **"Other people prevent me from reaching my goal."** At times we may feel that the only way to achieve what we want in life is if this person does this or if that person does that. And if we can only convince them to do what we want, life will be good again. Commitment is a step of personal responsibility. Leaving your life and its direction in the hands of others will never lead you to a life of intention because no one can manifest for you. In every moment you can make a decision to be happy or to be a victim, to create your own vision and choose your own energy or use others as your excuse to maintain a low energy. The decision you make is up to you alone. Do not look for someone else to be your hero. Be your own hero.

- **"I have too many goals, where do I start?"** Start where it feels right. I know that sounds simple, but when looking for the next best step, trust that taking inspired action is inviting the Universe to meet you where you are. If more than one desire lives in your heart, as you start to realize one dream, life will rearrange itself, bringing you closer to the other desires, even if at this time you are not working on them directly. Aligning your energy, as explained in the previous chapter, attracts your dreams, and taking action is an active invitation to the Universe. When the time comes, listen to inspiration and take the next best step.

Chapter 5

Step 4:
CURIOSITY

Understanding Fear
and Its Many Disguises

"Sandra, neither I nor my friends would ever hurt you on purpose."

I looked at the man in front of me in confusion. In relationships I always felt threatened, like people were out to get me. I felt like I could never let down my guard. So when my boyfriend, Finnegan, said those words, it seemed almost impossible to me. How could people not hurt me, and instead *want* to contribute to my happiness?

I got very curious about this, and the questions would not stop coming: How had I missed this for so long? Was this a thing? People wanted to be nice to others and make them happy without trying to hurt them on purpose?

Let me back up a bit.

It was a beautiful spring day in 2007. My boyfriend's friend and his wife had just bought a beautiful new town-home in Toronto. It had a great big terrace that overlooked the lake and the Toronto skyline. It was absolutely gorgeous. It was their first home, so as proud homeowners they invited their loved ones to celebrate this joyous occasion with a lovely barbecue. Their closest friends, including Finnegan and me, gathered to enjoy music, hamburgers, and a beautiful view.

Finnegan and I were dating and living on opposite sides of the city from each other, so we agreed to meet at his friend's place, which was halfway between our apartments. I wanted to make a good impression, so I decided to surprise the host with a dessert that was made in his hometown. However, I did not plan my time well and ended up arriving to the party quite late.

I proceeded to knock and ring the doorbell, but everyone was already outside on the terrace and didn't hear the bell. They didn't hear me yelling their names either. To make matter worse, my cell phone was dead, so I couldn't call.

So I did what any smart (not so much!) woman would do. I sat on their stoop and marinated in my own juices. I started to make up this whole story in my head about how my boyfriend was ignoring me, how he was disrespectful for not anticipating that I might be late, and how he wouldn't sacrifice his fun to wait for me in a place where I could easily reach him. I made up my own telenovela where I was the principal character, speaking out loud to myself about how miserable I was in life and groaning in frustration.

As time passed, I kept getting angrier. In my mind it was all his fault. I failed to see that the real problem was that I was late and didn't have a charged phone, both of which were my own fault. Instead, I sat there and wallowed in the "poor me" scenario and thought about how disrespectful he was.

Every now and then I would take a break from my victim role to once again ring the doorbell, knock on the door, and yell their names. Only to go back, with more fury, to my wallowing. I am sure that by this time, neighbors were probably starting to wonder about the woman in hysterics outside the new neighbors' townhouse. I was too busy living my own drama to notice.

Looking back, I can easily see that I could have done many things: I could have driven back to my place to recharge my phone and call, apologizing for being late and saying I was on my way. I could have driven to a nearby gas station and bought a charger so I could use my phone. I could have knocked on the neighbor's door so I could call out to my friends from the neighbor's terrace. But as is always the case when we play victim, we do the things that match our story, and apologizing or taking responsibility for the situation I found myself in . . . well, that did not play well with the pity party I was throwing for myself. So instead I wallowed in my own suffering.

Eventually, my boyfriend's friend came down to the kitchen to get something for the barbecue and heard the doorbell. When he opened the door, he said, smiling, "Lucky I came down, otherwise we may not have heard you." I told him that I had been at the door for at least 30 minutes. I proceeded then to go upstairs and make my disappointment heard.

Finnegan told me he had tried to get hold of me, but my phone was dead. When he offered me food, I loudly stated that "I was hungry 30 minutes ago when I first got here." When he said, "Sorry we didn't hear you," I again loudly shared my disappointment with him. In fact, I completely rained down on their party, making everyone uncomfortable. Even though I could have taken responsibility for my actions that led to the situation, then forgiven and forgotten and enjoyed myself, I was not a quitter; I couldn't let it go.

Once the party was over and we were alone, Finnegan said to me: "Sandra, neither I nor my friends would ever hurt you on purpose."

Those words made me pause. I wanted to cry from thinking that he cared enough about me that he would never hurt me on purpose; I wanted to cry because of the grief that I had gone through all of my life because I always expected to be hurt.

Uncovering Old Wounds

That was the very first time I remember becoming curious. I was so intrigued. I could not stop questioning: Was I creating the situations that led to the demise of my relationships? Is that why none of my relationships ever lasted past four months? Was I making assumptions about the people around me that matched a specific story I had in my head? Where did this story come from?

I probably spent a year after this day working on understanding the patterns around relationships in my life. Every time I would learn something new about how I saw relationships, I would once again bring myself to that state of open-minded curiosity and ask even more questions. My curiosity became like that thread that you pull on an old sweater only to see the whole thing start unraveling, yet you can't stop pulling. Every question led to an answer that then made me ask more questions. I witnessed how I behaved with Finnegan and others close to me. Whenever something that took away my peace showed up, I became curious and questioned what triggered it, what caused my behavior, and what came after the behavior. Through this never-ending questioning, a few things became clear about my own patterns in relationships.

Hurt was my expectation when it came to relationships. I carried the belief "no one can be trusted" with me into every relationship I had. Time and time again, my thought kept showing up as truth in my experience.

Life never turns out differently than what you expect. Once I recognized all the stories that I told myself about love, I realized that the behaviors they triggered in me were creating the demise of my own relationships.

When I looked at what triggered me to have those "poor me" and "bad you" episodes, I realized it was my fear of ending up alone and the belief that I did not deserve someone to love me. So when something happened that I could interpret as "yep, here I am, not lovable," it would poke at my old wound, and I would behave in a clingy, dramatic, and hurt way. Inside I was devastated because I thought the world was showing me time and time again that I was right all along, that I did not deserve to be loved.

Once I became aware of this, I could better manage when those triggers appeared, reminding myself that people were not out to get me. I could stop letting old wounds govern my life and my decisions and start taking control of my own life. I was for once in a position to stop living an unintended life and to start making every action I took an intended one.

I started working with my therapist, Elizabeth, to understand where that old wound came from. As is the case with most of our old wounds, mine started in childhood. Somehow as a child I made the decision that I was not worth loving, and as things happened in my life, I used them to reinforce that belief about myself. Then I proceeded to live based on that belief, especially in the area of romantic relationships, which is one of the areas where we are at our most vulnerable.

Also, I noticed my behaviors were consistent with the relationships I had witnessed as a child, including every telenovela I watched as a kid. As a child, I saw a lot of lack of respect, a lot of crying, and a lot of drama. I was replicating it all. I didn't know better. Once I recognized this, I started looking for different models around me because I wanted to learn what was actually possible in a relationship. I found one not too far from me. Finnegan's friends had a relationship based on respect, fun, and love. I became very curious again. I wanted to understand how a relationship could function without loud voices. It turns out it can, and it is beautiful.

I credit that day in the spring of 2007 with turning around how I viewed relationships. The more I witnessed my hurt and my immediate desire to act up, the more the hurt melted away. I became compassionate about the chica in me who believed that she didn't deserve love and slowly started to allow myself to be vulnerable, as only by showing myself fully would I be able to also experience love in all of its forms. I started to heal.

The Origins of Fear

When we first come into our physical experience, our factory setting (or default state) is peace. And anything that takes away our peace has its source in fear. However, we were not born with fear. Fear is actually a learned skill.

Think back to a toddler you may have seen lately, a little two- or three-year-old. If you observe them long enough, you'll notice that they are fearless. If they want to climb a chair, they don't doubt themselves, question what others would think, or believe they don't deserve to climb the chair. Instead, they let their desire guide them. They get their little legs and arms moving, climb the chair, and enjoy the view. That is our human nature. At our core, we are all invincible.

So how do we go from powerful and determined individuals in our toddler years to adults paralyzed with fear?

We all created stories about ourselves that were meant to keep us safe, and we let them build a wall around us that kept us away from anything that is uncertain and unknown. The voices in our head are the voices we heard as a child: "Don't do that or you will hurt yourself"; "Good girls don't do that"; "If you loved me you would be good"; and "¿Qué dirán?" ("What will people say?"). The people who said those things to us as children had good intentions. They wanted to show us how the world works, create boundaries, and keep us safe. The thing is, we let those voices become our own voices and then we allowed them to rule our life. Whenever a new situation appeared that seemed outside our comfort zone, we would hear those voices telling us we would get hurt and shy away from it. We wouldn't question them; we would just take them as truth and go with it.

A Course in Miracles says there are two emotions: love and fear. It also says that fear has many forms and is unique to the individual, yet all fears have the same source. Fear makes up stories in the person's head. Fear is the absence of love and it likes to live in the shadows, creating its own stories of dark intentions against us. When you shine a light on it, the fears will melt away and become small, no longer having a protagonist role in your life. Love and compassion are that light, and curiosity is the switch that will turn it on.

When anything happens in your life that takes away your peace, it's a time to get curious and ask yourself endless questions about what triggered it, what behaviors were caused by it, and what stories you are telling yourself.

Recognizing the Many Disguises of Fear

Fear does not like to be recognized. Like I said, it likes to live in the shadows and make up stories. So very often it will disguise itself as more acceptable manifestations. It will not show itself as "horror-movie monster is chasing me" paralyzing fear. Instead, it shows itself in a disguise that is easier to tolerate, yet helps you excuse your lack of action or self-reflection. Some of its disguises include:

- **Insecurity:** This happens when you convince yourself that you do not deserve the good in the world, certainly not the good that comes your way. When you feel insecure, you don't act, keeping yourself "safe" in a cocoon. You live small so that you do not find yourself wanting more than you believe you should have.

- **Superiority:** When you put others down, it allows you to think you are better, and better feels safer. It's a way for you to cope with your feelings that you are not enough. It's like role-playing without realizing you are stomping on others.

- **Laziness and procrastination:** When you know something needs to be done but you do not do it, it is a way to keep yourself safe. If you don't start the car, the car will never go, right? And so, you make yourself believe you are being lazy, when in reality you are scared.

- **Yeah . . . but:** If it smells like an excuse and sounds like an excuse, it's fear. You sometimes try to rationalize not doing or saying something, so you find ways to convince yourself that there is a perfectly rational reason not to do it.

- **Perfectionism:** I call it the analysis paralysis fear. Everything needs to be perfect for you to do something. But guess what? Life is never perfect, so you keep yourself safe by not marching on until all the i's are dotted and all the t's are crossed.

- **Avoidance:** Sometimes fear is so scary and hurts so much that it feels better if you don't look it in the face. You dance around it, but you don't dance with it.

- **Sadness:** This is when you swallow your fear. It is actually the healthiest of the disguises as long as you use it as a springboard to becoming curious about the feeling and its source. But when you make it your new default setting, it's just a way to paralyze yourself and create an anchor that keeps you from moving forward. Our culture also uses phrases such as Sé fuerte, mija (Be strong, my daughter) to push you to ignore your feelings and pretend they were never there.

- **Anger:** This is when you projectile vomit your fear. The fear is so agonizingly unpleasant that your body cannot stand it, so instead you let it all out and spill it on everyone and everything around you. You blame others for your situation because looking inside to see your role in what's happening is just too painful. At the core, though, there is always a very scared child who needs a hug.

- **People-pleasing:** When you let others take the wheel, you completely rescind any responsibility you have for the way your life turns out. It allows you to sit back and let others decide for you. It also helps you fish for compliments and get reassurance that you are "not that bad."

- **Extreme self-reliance:** When you walk away from others, saying you don't need anyone, you keep yourself safe from disappointment. If you believe people are not to be trusted and you can trust only yourself, you will find ways to keep yourself isolated from everyone.

- **Pride:** This is the armor of fear. You do not dare show your vulnerability for fear that you will be hurt. The unintended consequence, however, is that you isolate yourself from other feelings, such as love and compassion, as well.

The Unintended Consequences of Fear

Now that you are equipped to recognize fear, the next step is to become curious and recognize what triggers it and what behaviors it causes.

Like *A Course in Miracles* says, fear makes up stories about the world that only we know and believe. Because of this, fear creates a personal platform from which we make decisions and the lens with which we see our lives. This platform becomes our truth.

The issue with this is that when we make decisions from fear, we make decisions that will not necessarily be in line with what we want or who we are. Instead they are merely reactions. We end up living an unintended life. The *Course* also says, "Would you rather be right or would you rather be happy?" When we live from fear, being right becomes the only way to live, leaving happiness behind. When we are scared, we are fighting for our very own survival, just like early humans did when bears chased them. They had to fight for their lives with sticks and stones. Now our lives are not on the line, although it sometimes feels like it, and the bears are imagined.

And guess what? We do a lot of foolish stuff when we feel threatened. We hurt the people who love us, we leave jobs that are good for us, we spend money on things that give us reassurance, and we cause events to happen that hurt our chances of being happy.

There is a universal fear, a fear that is at the core of every disguise. That is the fear of not deserving to be loved. Everyone around us is dealing with a form of this fear, and the stories it makes up are about not being worthy. As children, we saw the world as a play happening around us—with ourselves as the protagonists in the center of it—so whenever something that hurt us happened, we assumed it was because of something we did, creating this belief that we were bad and did not deserve good. Once that lens was created in our lives, every event that took place was seen through that lens. My mom yelled because she was having a bad day? Surely it was my fault. My teacher rolled her eyes when I said good morning? Surely she hates me.

My boyfriend broke up with me after months of dating? Surely I don't deserve love. It is a fear we learned, yet it is so ingrained inside us that we can't remember a time when we didn't have it. It is the song that plays in our heads constantly, whether we are aware of it or not.

So when something takes away our peace, it is an opportunity to become curious, ask a lot of questions, and dig into that fear with compassion and understanding. Once love shines on that fear, it will no longer have power over us. Being curious about the triggers also helps us understand the stories we tell ourselves. Many times the problem is not the situation but the story we made up in our heads about the situation.

I remember when I was a child, I once saw an adult in a restaurant argue with the waiter over the way his eggs had been cooked. He likely had created this story in his head that the waiter was out to get him, and there was nothing the waiter could say to change that story, even though he tried. The fight escalated until the customer threw the plate against the wall, to the amazement of everyone in the restaurant. I remember seeing eggs on the wall and pieces of the shattered plate all over the floor while the man who had thrown the plate stood looking at the waiter with righteous indignation. I remember thinking, *Wow, that man really loves his eggs.* Now I know no one loves eggs that much. Somehow that man was creating these stories in his head about people being out to get him, and getting those eggs cooked in a way he did not like confirmed the story and triggered him to behave in a way that was almost unconscious, just like I behaved when I told myself the story about my boyfriend not wanting to open the door for me at the barbecue. I made it all about how he was disrespecting me, not loving me enough, and not seeing me. When in reality he just could not hear the doorbell ring.

Author Byron Katie says, "Reality is always kinder than the stories we tell about it." Stories can also be irrational, because when we think a thought for long enough, we come to believe it is true—no questions asked.

Many years ago, my friend Laura and I were having dinner with a friend of ours. We were catching up and having a great time. Toward the end of the meal, our friend stretched his arms up, reaching for the sky. He must have been tired from a long day, yet Laura and I unconsciously flinched away.

Having grown up in Mexico, Laura and I learned from our families that if you stretched at the table your guts would explode. I am unable to tell you where this folktale came from, but here we were, two grown women in our 30s flinching when someone stretched at the table because we truly believed we would end up with guts all over us. Irrational stories cannot be explained, yet nonetheless we let them rule our decisions and behaviors.

Think about how fear and our irrational stories drive us to hurt others. In the story about the eggs, a man was turning his hurt onto a waiter. But what if our fear causes us to hurt the people we love the most? Our parents, our partners, our kids.

Our kids are of serious concern in this situation. When they are little, their experiences create the lens they will use to understand life. Yet when we let our fears get in the way of our relationships with them, we are hurting them and helping them create the belief that life hurts, just as we learned from our parents, and our parents learned from their own parents. It reminds me of the telenovela called

Cadenas de Amargura (*Chains of Bitterness*). Fear is the gift that keeps on giving.

Chica, make the decision that you will cut that chain. You will be the one to wake up from this dream and see life for what it is. You will return to your factory setting of peace.

Steps 1 to 3 in this book show you how to create the life you want; Step 4 shows you how to awaken and keep that life you created. Step 5 will help you heal those wounds so you can live your life in freedom.

It's easy to create good in your life just to lose it soon after. This happens because we let our fears rule us. Our decisions and our behaviors take us down the path of reactionary decisions that take us away from what we want.

Curiosity will help you take the wheel once again. Be curious about the reasons behind anything that takes away your peace, about what triggered it, and about what behaviors it caused. Never stop asking questions. Be curious at all times. Learn about yourself and what makes you tick, for when you do this you will start to live a life that is in alignment with your human nature and with what you truly want.

Curiosity will also help you understand others and the fears they are dealing with. You will be able to take things a little less personally and understand that everyone has an irrational fear they are living with, often the fear that they are not deserving of love. Help heal this wound in the world by giving love and compassion to those who do not think they deserve it, instead of responding with your own fear.

Do not let the relationships in your life be about two people's wounds interacting with one another. Take off the disguise, show yourself—vulnerability and all—and you will be amazed at how your life turns around and shows you peace instead.

Don't get me wrong, I recognize that dancing with your fears is scary as the ghost of *La Llorona*. Being vulnerable feels extremely threatening. But believe me, the alternative is a lot scarier. Be brutally honest and brave. The following exercises will help you do just that. However, if as you do these exercises you find the fear is too big to tolerate or face by yourself, gently allow yourself to feel the enormity of the feeling and seek help from a professional. It will be one of the biggest acts of love you can do for yourself.

¿Y Cómo?

The Onion Exercise

The objective of this exercise is to peel back the layers of your fear in order to disarm it. Once you recognize the stories you tell yourself, you can then examine the places in your life where you learned those stories and the voices behind them.

Start by finding a time when you will not be interrupted and a place where you can be by yourself. Decide at the beginning of this exercise that you will be honest—brutally honest.

Observe a recent event in your life where you lost your peace, had a violent outburst, or had so much emotion that it took you out of commission for a while. It is best if the exercise is done within 24 hours of that event taking place. This exercise will allow you to peel back the layers. The following diagram will help. You can download the template for this exercise at www.sandrahinojosaludwig.com/chicawhynot.

Where did I learn this:

Start by writing the first feeling you feel on the first line. This is the outer layer of the onion. Write whatever comes first. Then get very curious about that feeling and ask yourself, *Why do I feel this way?* Write that answer on the second line. That is the second layer of the onion. Ask yourself again, *Why do I feel this way?* Don't hold back your emotions. Let them come to the surface, feel them, close your eyes, and cry or scream if needed, but do not avoid them. Get right in there with them. Continue down as many layers as you need to until you exhaust your answers. Then breathe. And see what you wrote.

Now that you can see it all on paper, get curious again. Where did you learn those stories? Do they have a voice you can recognize? Whose voice is it? Write it down in the reflection space under the onion. See the stories for what they are—stories that were never true.

As an example, this is my Onion Exercise for the story I shared at the beginning of this chapter:

I think my boyfriend did this on purpose because he does not love me.

Sooner or later, all my boyfriends get tired of me and try to make me leave.

All my relationships fail. Relationships hurt.

I can't keep a man.

I don't deserve a relationship.

I don't deserve to be loved.

I am not lovable.

Where did I learn this:

At a young age, I learned through being punished for things I did wrong that I only deserve love if I am "good." I learned I am not good. I don't deserve love. It is the voice of my parents.

I learned that relationships involve a lot of yelling, crying, and sometimes violence. I learned that hurt is a normal part of a relationship. I learned this from the adult relationships around me and from telenovelas.

Now that you have uncovered this fear, continue on with your life while looking for it to arise. See once again what triggers it. Compare what you see with what you have written and add to the Onion Exercise as needed. As you repeat this exercise over and over, the fear will start losing its grip. You will begin to anticipate when triggers will show up in your life, and you'll be able to respond with an intentional thought rather than react in a disproportionate way to the event, in an almost unconscious, out-of-control manner because the triggers have poked a place within you that is hurt and fearful. As you become familiar with the hurt at the root of your fear, use the exercises in the next chapter, Step 5: Compassion, to compassionately address it and help it heal.

The Unknowns and Facts Exercise

The objective of this exercise is to highlight what is real, what is unknown, and what is a made-up story. Many times, there are unknowns that you perceive as threats and which cause you anxiety. When you think about them, you'll be able to identify the small number of these that are actual real threats you need to deal with. But many other unknowns are just made-up monsters that you believe are out to get you, though they have no real chance of hurting you. This exercise helps you distinguish between the two.

If the Onion Exercise was too intense for you, do this exercise before re-attempting the Onion Exercise. Then when you feel comfortable, go back to the Onion Exercise. Remember, avoidance is a disguise that fear wears. You can't dance around your fears for too long; eventually you need to dance with them. This exercise is like the gentle cumbia before the sexy tango.

Start by finding a time when you will not be interrupted and a place where you can be by yourself. Decide at the beginning of this exercise that you will be honest—brutally honest. Do not let the stories you tell yourself become your truth. Question everything.

In the "My Story and Feelings" section, write your story about a situation that happened when you were upset and how it made you feel. Then move to the box that says "Facts." What are the facts behind the stories you tell yourself? Only facts go in here: no conclusions, unknowns, or assumptions, just facts. Do not include things that people tell you are facts; include only facts you have evidence for. Once the facts are laid out, think back to the situation. Are there any unknowns that could turn into real risks and threats you should be aware of or prepared for? Write them down in the "Unknowns" box.

Use the diagram below to write down your conclusions. You can download the template for this exercise at www.sandrahinojosaludwig.com /chicawhynot.

My Story and Feelings:

Facts	Unknowns

Once you complete this chart, look at each item under Unknowns and ask yourself: *Is it a real threat?* If the answer is yes, then ask yourself, *How can I mitigate or eliminate this threat?*

For example, if your story is that you will inevitably get into a car accident and be paralyzed, and this makes you feel so fearful of driving that you do not ever want to leave your home, you can start by looking at the facts. How often do you get in accidents? What are the actual accident statistics in your area? Are you a bad driver? Is the weather so bad that the risk of an accident is high? Then look at the unknowns and decide if they could become real threats. An unknown could be something other drivers could do. If you drive often there is a chance, however small, that you could get in an accident because of something someone else does. But there are ways to mitigate that threat. Some measures you could adopt include making sure that you have good tires, that your car is maintained regularly, that you do not drive under the influence of drugs or alcohol, and that you do not text and drive.

As an example, this is my Unknowns and Facts Exercise for the story I shared at the beginning of this chapter:

My Story and Feelings:

I think my boyfriend did this on purpose because he does not love me. If he did, he would have noticed I was not there ye and tried to get in touch with me or look for me. At the very least, he would have stayed in a part of the house where he could hear me ring the bell.

Facts	Unknowns
• He did not know I would be late and my phone would be dead.	Does he love me?
• There was no way for him to get in touch with me.	
• He called my phone, but it had no battery.	
• He was with his friends.	
• He trusted I was an adult who could take care of herself.	

As you can see, there was an unknown: *Does he love me?* Once I identified this unknown, I found ways to analyze it to understand if it had a real chance to become a threat. If it had a chance, I could then find ways to mitigate or eliminate that threat.

In this case, I could deal with the unknown either by asking him directly or by observing him. I knew I had a trigger about relationships, so I decided to observe instead of asking my boyfriend directly, as I knew this would create a whole new set of stories for me to analyze. Instead, I observed how he treated me. It was not long until I knew his love for me was a fact rather than an unknown. A few years later, he became my husband.

The Sphere Exercise

The objective of this exercise is to very gently start feeling your fear. This exercise is geared toward people who cannot name a fear or a story. In my practice, I have come across this kind of scenario a few times. The client was able to express only the dissatisfaction, sadness, anger, or anxiety but was unable to articulate what was behind that feeling. Sometimes our fears are so massive that even touching them causes too much pain. In these cases, a very gentle approach helps. If the Onion Exercise was a tango, and the Unknowns and Facts Exercise was a cumbia, this is a waltz—you know, arms stretched out, barely touching, with very slow music to move to.

Start by finding a time when you will not be interrupted and a place where you can be by yourself. Decide at the beginning of this exercise that you will be brave and will see this exercise through. If you would like to access this exercise as a pre-recorded guided meditation, you can find it at www.sandra hinojosaludwig.com/chicawhynot.

Find a comfortable spot where you can be seated—either on a couch or on a pillow on the floor. Close your eyes. Breathe in and out. Focus completely on your breath and follow its rhythm. Slowly take your attention from your breath and remember the event that took place where you lost control. See every detail. What were you wearing? Where were you standing? Who was around you? What was said? Listen to it and check in with your gut. What are you feeling? Very gently remember your behavior. What was that feeling underneath that behavior?

Stay with that feeling. Gently locate the feeling. Is it in your chest? Your stomach? Your neck? Your head? Where is it?

Keep feeling it. What shape is it? Is it a sphere, a cube, any other shape?

Keep feeling it. If at any time you lose the feeling, remember once again the situation and capture it again. What color is it?

Keep feeling it. Does it say anything? If so, what is it saying? Repeat it out loud. Whose voice is it?

If you are unable to hear it speak, stay with it. Feel it in your body where you located it, keep seeing its shape and its color. Get closer to it.

What is the feeling? Is it sadness? Anger? Describe it out loud. Touch it. What does it feel like? See it. It is in you, but it is not you. It is finite within yourself.

Once you become very familiar with it, hug yourself by wrapping your arms around the part of your body where the feeling is. Send it love. Tell it that everything will be okay. Recognize its hurt. Tell it you are there to make sure everything is okay.

Continue hugging yourself. Do not stop your feelings from coming. Let them flow. Hug yourself until the feeling reveals more of itself or feels less sharp. Breathe. Open your eyes when you are ready.

If the fear spoke to you, write what it told you in the Onion Exercise or in the Unknowns and Facts Exercise and try to complete those exercises. If it did not talk to you, continue this exercise every time there is something significant that takes away your peace. Eventually it will talk to you. At that time, proceed to the Onion Exercise or the Unknowns and Facts Exercise. Be gentle; there is no rush. But keep trying.

Sí, Pero

- **"I can't name the fear or its source."** Remember that perfectionism is also a disguise that fear can wear. Don't go for perfect, go for good enough. Try the Sphere Exercise. Whenever you have more information, go on to either the Unknowns and Facts Exercise or the Onion Exercise. Do not use this as your excuse to not face your fear. Even recognizing that there is something taking away your peace is good enough to start shining some light on that fear. If the fear feels too big, ask for help from a licensed professional. Stay with it.

- **"I can't control my reaction when triggers appear."** This may be true when you are unconsciously reacting to a trigger and a fear you are not aware of. But as soon as you recognize there is something taking away your peace, you have the consciousness to control how you respond. You are an adult and can control your response. If the feeling is too overwhelming, simply recognize that you need some time alone and remove yourself from the situation. Remember that whatever you say or do cannot be undone, ever. Be mindful of the wake you leave behind you. And above all, do not blame others for how you react. It is always you, 100 percent you.

- **"I realized too late when a fear bubbled up to the surface and made me take an unwanted action."** You can't turn back the clock. It's okay, though. First of all, recognize that there was a fear and a trigger. Complete any of the exercises listed here that are within your level of comfort. Shine light on the fear. Now take responsibility for your actions, and apologize sincerely. You can't take back what you said or did. Apologize in a way that is comfortable for the person or people you hurt. Once you have apologized, do not continue to beat yourself up over it. Focus on the learning rather than on the mistake, and compassionately forgive yourself.

Chapter 6

Step 5:
COMPASSION

Be Gentle with Yourself

"I love food."

This is what I always answer when people ask me how and why I became a food scientist. Most times they respond with a conspiring grin, as if saying, "I know what you mean, yum!" But for me, my love for food is more than that. I love it so much that in high school I decided to become a food scientist. This led me to dedicate 22 years of my life to bringing delicious food to people and pets.

And the truth is, I do love food. Very much. I love the texture, the flavor, the complexity, and the science behind it, down to the molecular level. I love the friendships I have developed through my love of food, and the career accomplishments I have achieved because of my love of food. Food is right at the center of my life. Food has been with me in the good times and in the bad times. Food, for a long time, was the love of my life.

What I don't tell people is that food has also been my poison of choice.

Let me back up a bit.

I have, for as long as I can remember, always been overweight. Sometimes the extra weight is just a cute couple of pounds that makes me a bit rounder, but other times it has been extreme weight that has affected my ability to move and the way I interact with life, both physically and emotionally. The extra weight has at times made me think twice about going on a trip, going to a party, or going on a date. Sometimes, it has been my excuse to live life from the sidelines instead of living life to the fullest.

The first memory I have is of being in kindergarten, sitting on the floor in a circle with my classmates, and my teacher pointing at me and laughing because I looked like a ball. All my classmates were laughing with her, and I remember wishing I would disappear.

I probably did look like a ball! When I was growing up in Mexico, no building had heating. And, of course, coming from a warm country, the moment the temperature hit 15 degrees Celsius (59°F) we dressed as if we were going on an excursion to the arctic, with hat, gloves, thermal socks, and all. I was probably wearing seven layers and could barely bring my arms down to my sides. So yes, I probably looked like a ball, but regardless, being mocked for looking like a ball made me cringe.

This was the first of many instances in my life when my weight and appearance were a sore reminder that I did not fit in and that people looked at me and saw fat.

This kind of mocking continued all through my schooling up to university, where near the end of my bachelor's program I received the prize for the best butt. Surely it was a joke to everyone about the size of my butt, but not for me. Walking up to the podium to pick up that "prize" without crying in front of all my laughing classmates was a great achievement.

The struggle with my weight was (and sometimes still is) the biggest presence in my life, the constant noise in my head. It's the thing that is constantly being added to my every thought: *I love that dress! (But I'll bet it would look terrible on me.) I would love to travel to Australia! (But will people stare at me because I am so fat?*, followed by me Googling how many fat people live in Australia.) *I wish I could be a runner. (Are you kidding me? You'll be out of breath in the first two minutes.) I love these tamales! (Of course you do.)*

It's not like I haven't tried. I started dieting at 14, restricting my food as a way to have some sort of control over this part of my life. Over the years I have probably lost close to 250 pounds total, only to gain it right back every time. I know every diet and have tried every exercise. I am a pro at losing weight. I am like a walking nutritional and fitness library. I can tell you the calories in most foods and the rules of every diet from keto to paleo to low fat, and I can tell you which exercise to do to tackle each muscle group. And yet I always gain the weight right back.

That's when the shaming and blaming starts. I call myself all sorts of names, then to convince myself to be someone else, someone who does not run to food all the time and who can keep from bingeing and can stop the cycle.

It has been my life's work to overcome this.

Throughout my life, I've always been an achiever. As we say in Mexico, "Donde pongo el ojo, pongo la bala" ("Where I put my eye, I put the bullet"). I have always pushed myself beyond my comfort zones and fears to achieve anything I want. And this has led me to create a beautiful life for myself. I am an expert at pushing through with determination and grit. I am filled with an energy that achieves, pushes, motivates, and keeps me going even after I run out of fuel.

Yet my weight has always been the area that I can't seem to figure out, and even this achieving energy cannot help me here. Because the moment this energy pushes me, I hide from it and sabotage myself.

So in 2016 I decided I would not "push through." I would not "do it, no matter what." And I would certainly not just "get over it." I would, this time, try to love and support myself as a best friend, instead of being a drill sergeant pushing myself to follow instructions as I worked to lose weight. Instead of pursuing the energy that creates worlds, I would summon the energy that nurtures the world. The energy of love.

As a result, curiosity, as explained in Chapter 5, has become my everyday practice to understand why I use food in my life. Because of this, food has also been my greatest teacher.

I learned that I eat when I have big emotions, both positive and negative. Food grounds me. It makes me feel safe and numb when life gets scary because of big sadness, anger, anxiety, and even happiness. Happiness makes me scared because I am also recovering from my stories that consistently tell me I am not deserving of happiness. Food numbs me through it all. It makes a scary world manageable.

I eat when I am bored, or as a procrastination tool. Food is the thing I do when I don't know what to do, or I don't want to do what I know needs to be done. It is my distraction of choice. I also use food as a way to show love. Anyone who has ever come to my home knows how much I love cooking and feeding my loved ones. In Mexican households, food is always at the center of every celebration and milestone. The kitchen is always the gathering place where we connect. So it is tradition for me to continue to use food as a central piece of my life. "I see you. I love you. Here, have a chile en nogada."

So, after realizing that nothing would change until I did, in my 40s I tried a new thing called compassion. I figured pushing myself had not worked too well for me, so I would try something else. I would compassionately love and support myself through this.

While curiosity helps us see what is creating our suffering, compassion is the action that follows the learning. Compassion is the active part of love. Compassion is the skill that helps us reach for more in a way that feels safe and loving. After all, it's hard to grow and evolve into our best self when internally we keep berating, shaming, and blaming ourselves for our shortcomings.

I started to be gentle with myself and allow myself to grieve when I fell, to celebrate when I did great, to ask for help when I couldn't figure out which steps to take next, to surrender and ask for help from the Universe when I felt defeated.

I am now learning to treat myself like a best friend would. I do this by holding myself when I feel sadness, listening to myself when I feel anger, giving myself mercy when I fall once again, loving myself, and being present when I feel like I have reached the end of myself, like I can't go any further.

I am learning to recognize that I am not my decisions. I am the manifestation of the Universe in a physical form, and because of this I deserve love unconditionally from myself. By loving myself, it is easier to recognize my role in making decisions that took me away from my goals. And I give myself permission to act differently.

I still hold myself accountable for my choices, but I do it with a different lens—one of curiosity and learning that allows me to grow from my failures.

By trying to understand what is beneath my need to numb, I am also learning that on all occasions hunger is never the pain I experience, and therefore food is never the solution. I am learning to cope in a way that truly helps me through whatever I am going through in a constructive way.

Now my path feels gentler. I'm still climbing that mountain, but I feel like I have put my baggage down. I am doing it now without carrying regret, guilt, shame, anger, disappointment, and denial. Instead, I fill myself with acceptance, mercy, love, and understanding. I give myself permission to breathe and be human. That is the fuel that will get me to the top of the mountain.

I have also sought help from others. I have surrounded myself with a therapist and a support group who understand me and help me navigate my emotions when I need it most. They lovingly advise me when I run out of ideas, and lovingly hold me accountable and help me redirect when I sabotage myself. I am not doing this alone anymore. And it feels good to walk the path with others by my side. I am being there for myself.

And as I started to do this, the Universe started supporting me on my path and revealing things to me that make my path easier to walk. In 2016, I was diagnosed with lipedema, a disorder where fat deposits occur under the skin, affecting mainly the limbs. In my case, it affects my legs. Lipedema is incurable, painful, and progressive, and not affected by diet or exercise. The cause is unknown but is most likely hereditary and hormonal. I have been dealing with this disease since puberty.

I spent years fighting my body, without knowing my body was struggling.

This new knowledge has helped me to be even softer with my body, and to try to help it in any way I can. Besides feeding myself foods that help my body be its best, I am now taking on activities that help my lymphatic system (which is impacted by the disease) be as healthy as it can be. I do yoga and water exercises and have enlisted a fantastic massage therapist who provides me with therapy that helps drain my lymphatic system and keep it running.

I am now my body's best friend.

I may always be tempted by food and its ability to numb big emotions. And that is okay.

This journey is not about perfection. It's about resilience and accepting my humanity. It's about loving myself and giving myself the space to be the best version of me, not because I push myself endlessly, but because I reveal and celebrate my true nature, and as a consequence, the true me is no longer afraid to shine and live life and feel all of its big emotions. I now feel free to live life to its fullest.

Food is the love of my life, my poison of choice, my tool for achieving numbness, my distraction, and my biggest teacher. Food is my sticky place.

The Sticky Place

We all have a sticky place. For me it's food and my weight. For you it might be abundance, health, career, relationships, or self-worth.

We all have a thing (or two or three).

The sticky place is that area of your life you have spent the most energy unsuccessfully trying to overcome. You work, you study, you dedicate yourself, yet every milestone feels like climbing a mountain, and a slippery mountain at best! Because just when you feel you may for once reach that summit that you have been visualizing for years, something happens and you lose the momentum you had, you tumble down the mountain, and you find yourself, once again, starting all over.

Time and time again, you feel defeated.

A sticky place can be recognized by one or more of the following elements:

- It makes you feel shame.

- It brings out judgment from within you.

- It's hard to share with others.

- You downplay its effect on your life.

- You may even pretend it isn't there.

- When you are truthful, you notice it is the constant noise in your head.

- It constantly adds itself to any statements of dreams and hopes to prevent you from dreaming big or living life to its fullest (e.g., "I would love to take a vacation to the beach, but how can I if I never have any money?").

- It feels like you can never achieve the outcome you desire, no matter how hard you work at it.

- It feels like hopelessness.

- It makes you angry with yourself.

The sticky place is the quicksand of the emotional world.

During my own experience dealing with my sticky place, I have learned that just as in dealing with quicksand, sudden movements and panicking never helps, and powering through only keeps you stuck and makes you sink faster.

The only way out is allowing yourself to remain calm and breathe, make yourself lighter by removing extra baggage, and proceed to make slow and intentional movements to get yourself back to the surface so that you can set yourself free.

Patience is key. Results may not be immediate, and at times you may find yourself sinking again. Breathe and start again. One step at a time.

When you are dealing with a sticky place, approach it just like quicksand: You need to remain calm and breathe. Make yourself lighter by letting go of the guilt, regret, and shame you have carried your whole life around this particular area. You also become lighter by embracing all of the fear and the pain that caused the sticky place in the first place.

Being curious helps you shed some light on what it is that you are trying to numb. Compassion helps you lovingly stop your dependence on your sticky place as a coping mechanism.

As you slowly start to heal your pain, you can take a few small intentional steps to once again regain your ground. By being patient, you realize that the sticky place has something to teach you, and the lesson must be learned before you can overcome it. And that may take time. Only curiosity and compassion will help with overcoming your sticky place. They will set you free.

The Three Pillars of Compassion

Overcoming your sticky place is a process in which actions and motivation alone don't deliver results unless they are paired with lots of love and support and a fundamental change in your thoughts around this area of your life. You must move from shame to acceptance, from ignoring the wound to giving it love, from blaming to mercy. This change in perspective can be achieved by using the pillars of compassion: honoring yourself, embracing your feelings, and asking for help.

Here are how the pillars can be executed in your life:

PILLAR 1: HONOR YOURSELF

Compassion starts with acceptance. This is acceptance of what is and of what you may have contributed to get you where you are. It is not about blaming but about accepting reality, as author Byron Katie would encourage. When you don't accept, you are constantly spending your energy wishing things would be different. Honoring yourself also means being true to yourself and your needs. Here are some specific ways you can honor yourself:

- **Be true and accept yourself.** Listen to your soul. It is said that the soul knows the way. When your soul asks you to take on a loving and supporting action such as resting, eating well, moving your body, saving money, seeking expertise, setting up clear boundaries, etc. and you don't, you are abandoning yourself. And that feels like betrayal. If this occurs, don't avoid this fact, but don't judge it either. Accept it for what it is and know there is some fear behind this sabotage that you need to work through. Become curious about it and learn from it. Turn perceived failures into learning and growing opportunities. If a path seems to no longer serve you, your soul will gently prompt you to change paths. Listen to it and softly switch strategies as needed. Know that the Universe's wisdom and power lives inside of you.

Gain new clarity and open yourself to collaboration from the Universe while executing your commitment. But at the same time, connect with yourself by practicing the curiosity to understand your triggers and fears, as well as by practicing the compassion for your journey and for the very scared kid, teen, and adult behind your sticky place.

- **Create a safe space inside and outside yourself.** Many times your sticky place cannot fully be exposed without you feeling vulnerable. You don't accept it, you won't share it with anyone else, and, even worse, you use it as your excuse for believing you do not deserve better, staying in places and situations that do not serve you well. You bury your head in the sand. You tiptoe around it. But you never make eye contact with it except to judge it and shame it.

  Honor this very wounded place inside of you by first admitting to yourself that it exists, by becoming curious about it, by listening to it and what it has to say without judgment, and by saying to it, "I hear you, I love you, we will do this together." Allow yourself to experience unconditional love toward yourself—warts and all, sticky place and all.

  It also helps to honor this sticky place by sharing it with people who have earned your trust and love you without judgment. In our culture we say that la ropa sucia se lava en casa (dirty laundry is taken care of at home), but when it comes to the sticky place, a support system can make a huge difference. Know that the people in your inner circle will love you no matter what, sticky place and all.

Author Dr. Edith Eva Eger says, "Expression is the opposite of depression." Let your sticky place breathe.

Also honor yourself by removing from your life those people who project their own fears and perceptions onto you, for they will not help you. Create a community of people who will be by your side no matter what, and remove yourself from those who will hurt you physically and/or emotionally. Honor your worth by allowing yourself to exist in a safe space, and do not accept anything less.

When you start to allow yourself to receive unconditional love from you and your inner circle and stand by your worth, you will be safe and free to let go of false expectations of what you "should be." Accepting yourself as you are is, after all, the first step toward healing.

- **Differentiate a supporting action from an indulging action.** Honoring and being good to yourself does not mean indulging. It does not mean eating the churro when it's not aligned with your goals of a healthy body, or buying the shoes when doing so does not allow you to meet your financial goal of being debt-free, or going for the chisme (gossip) when you are trying to bring peace into your existence. Recognize and differentiate between supporting and indulging. Supporting may feel like depriving yourself in the short term, but it gives you joy and pride once you achieve your goals. Indulging, on the other hand, may feel good immediately, but it brings shame afterward because it moves you away from what you seek.

PILLAR 2: EMBRACE YOUR FEELINGS

Once you have honored yourself, you can then feel safe to embrace your feelings as they are, free of judgment or expectations. As you do that, you start to surround your inner self with love. You can embrace your feelings by doing the following:

- **Grieve.** Recognize that the sticky place feels big and overwhelming. It is, after all, fear manifesting itself as sadness and anger. Recognize it and let it come out. Don't shy away from it. It may feel big and it may hurt like hell, but it will not kill you. Cry for the pain this sticky place has caused in your life, cry for the times you failed and abandoned yourself, and cry because of the pain and fear that is behind the sticky place. Cry until you have no more tears. And then tell yourself how much you love yourself and allow the presence of the divine to fill your heart with hope and love. And breathe.

- **Celebrate.** There will be times when you realize you are miles away from where you started, and other times only steps away from where you started. Celebrate regardless. Put on your favorite salsa music and dance yourself senseless, treat yourself to a walk in a beautiful place, or sing out loud to Thalia in the shower or in the car. This is you rewarding yourself, recognizing how amazing you are, and loving yourself no matter how quickly (or slowly) you grow. Any growth is cause for celebration. By gathering the evidence in your life that you are capable of anything you set your mind to, you can gain the confidence to tackle bigger things. Be proud of yourself. Shining looks good on you.

• **Be patient.** Move at a pace that feels gentle, and do not give up. Sometimes pretending the sticky place does not exist feels easier and provides temporary relief. Other times, blaming yourself for not being where you wish you could be feels like a way to cope with the pain. But know that neither of these options will help it heal. Instead, pushing against it and burying your head in the sand makes the sticky place bigger and bigger over time. The compassionate action here is working through this at a pace that feels safe so that you can set yourself free. Be patient. It may take you a lifetime. That's okay. What matters is moving in the right direction toward freedom.

PILLAR 3: ASK FOR HELP

Sticky places do not ever feel like small challenges to overcome. Instead, at times they feel too big to handle by yourself. If they feel that way, it's because most likely they are. Sometimes the most compassionate thing you can do for yourself is to ask for help. Here are some ways to ask for help:

- **Do research.** Start by seeking out people who have overcome what you are trying to overcome and ask them or research how they did it. Social media has become a great tool to find communities of people going through the same things as you. Imitating is not only a form of flattery for the person we imitate, but it is a very smart step on our part. By recognizing the footprints of those who have walked the path before us, we gain new perspective on what is possible and form a list of the things to consider as we walk our own path. Use their road map not because it is exactly the solution to your problems, but because it points you in the right direction.

- **Seek the help of professionals.** When looking for help, consider your physical, emotional, and energetic needs, as my friend Beth reminded me once, and make sure those are all met. Help for the physical you can come from massage therapists, fitness trainers, osteopaths, naturopaths, chiropractors, yoga instructors, certified TRE (trauma release exercises) instructors, dietitians, etc. Help for the emotional you can come from therapists, Inner Bonding facilitators, coaches who focus on self-love, members of the clergy, etc. Help for the energetic you can come from reiki practitioners, acupuncturists, angel healers, flower healers, energy healers, etc. If it feels scary to face your fears, don't do it alone. Make sure you have a team walking the path with you.

- **Surrender.** Sometimes the sticky place feels very overwhelming and big. It can feel insurmountable. When this happens, it's okay to fall to your knees and pray for guidance. When you surrender control of the outcome around your sticky place, you allow the Universe to take over and show you an easier path. It creates miracles in your life.

Moving Past the Sticky Place

Please know that the sticky place is not a punishment. It is instead a loving gift from the Universe to remind you of the call to be more. Accept this gift and the growth that comes from working through it compassionately. You have what it takes, and I can assure you, once you start gaining new perspective, you will see that confronting the sticky place is much better than continuing to ignore it.

Once when I lived in a small village in England after the birth of our son, my husband and I would take walks on Sunday mornings, pushing his stroller through our village. We loved those walks. We would walk by the old village church with its haunting graveyard, by sheep pasturing in emerald-green fields, by beautiful trees with colorful flowers, and by the old village pub filled with locals. Our walks were filled with conversations about our life and our future as we ate local pastries and smelled the moist soil in the fields. We thought our walks couldn't be any better.

There was, however, a big hill we always avoided. It just didn't seem worth it to climb it pushing a stroller because everything else was so beautiful and easy. The hill was up a paved road, with houses on both sides. It didn't seem as captivating as everything we had experienced so far.

But one day we got really curious about the hill. We kept asking ourselves: Could there be something worth seeing? And so, we decided to go up. We struggled on our way up, as it was quite steep, and pushing a stroller didn't make the endeavor any easier. We could feel ourselves starting to sweat and even wondered if we should go back, but we decided to keep going. We felt we had to see what was on top of it. To our surprise, when we got to the top, we found beautiful lavender fields and a view that was worth the climb. The lavender was arranged in beautiful rows of purple that seemed to go for miles and rejoice under the sun. We could see the North Sea not too far from us and our beautiful village below us with its church towers reaching tall toward the sky. We could see fields of all shades of green divided by winding narrow rural roads with hardly any cars on them. We could smell the purple of the lavender.

After that first climb, that hill became our favorite part of our Sunday walks.

In the same way, your sticky place will also reveal its beauty in your life when you take on the climb with compassion. It will feel like a struggle, and at times you may wonder why bother, but once you get to the top, what you discover will become a transformational milestone in your life.

Allow yourself that gift. You deserve it. The following exercises will help you find that beauty.

¿Y Cómo?

The Color Exercise

The objective of this exercise is to identify the big hills in your life where you will need this step as a foundation of your journey.

Start by finding a time when you will not be interrupted and a place where you can be by yourself. Decide at the beginning of this exercise that you will be honest—brutally honest.

Go back to the Bubble Exercise from Chapter 2. Review it again and notice if there is any area of your life that you may have omitted. If you did, add it to the exercise, with as much detail as possible. Keep in mind that the fact that you avoided adding it to your chart the first time may be an indication of it being a sticky place in your life. Look at all the bubbles within your chart. Feel your way through each of them and look for one or more of the following elements:

- It makes you feel shame.
- It brings out judgment from within you.
- It is hard to share with others.
- You downplay its effect on your life.
- You pretend it isn't there.
- When you are truthful, you notice it is the constant noise in your head.
- It constantly adds itself to any statements of dreams and hopes to prevent you from

dreaming big or living life to its fullest (e.g., "I would love to vacation at the beach! But how can I if I never have any money?").

- It feels like you can never achieve the outcome you desire no matter how hard you work at it.
- It feels like hopelessness.
- It makes you angry at yourself.

Now color each bubble with a color that resembles the intensity of the feelings you feel. The darker and more intense the color, the closer it is to being a sticky place. When you're finished, look at the chart. What areas jump out at you as the darker ones? Were you aware of those areas carrying so much energy?

Now that you have recognized those areas as the potential sticky places in your life, be curious and start slowly and compassionately working through them. In the exercise below, create a self-love and compassion plan for each one of those areas.

Self-Love and Compassion Practice

The objective of this exercise is to help you create a practice of self-love and compassion that fits in your life and will allow you to become intentional about supporting yourself through the sticky places you've identified.

Start by finding a time when you will not be interrupted and a place where you can be by yourself. Decide at the beginning of this exercise that you will approach it without judgment and instead see it with a lens of self-love, support, and compassion for yourself, the way you would advise your best friend going through a situation that is difficult. Create a plan for each one of the areas of intensity you uncovered in The Color Exercise in this chapter. Do one at a time using the following chart. You can download the template for this exercise at www.sandrahinojosa ludwig.com/chicawhynot.

Sticky Place: _____

Action	Plan
Honor Yourself	
Embrace Your Feelings	
Ask for Help	

Fill in each row with a clear plan that consists of compassionate, loving, judgment-free, supportive actions that you will take as you work through your sticky place. Although not included, it is implied that you have decided you will work on your sticky place. Ignoring it or pretending that it doesn't exist is not loving.

Here is how to fill in the chart:

Under Honor Yourself:

- Write what loving and supportive action your sticky place is asking of you. This may be an act of self-love or a boundary that you need to set. If it is also asking for a change in your path, write it down.

- Write the actions you will take to create a safe place both inside and outside yourself.

- Write down what indulging actions you have taken disguised as self-love, and instead write what supporting actions you will take.

Under Embrace Your Feelings:

- Write down the events or situations you want to recognize as areas of loss around your sticky place. Give yourself permission to grieve them, whether by yourself or with the help of someone who will listen without judgment—either a great friend or a licensed professional such as a therapist.

- Write down some important milestones and how you will celebrate them.

- Write a statement of how you will allow yourself to work on this and at what pace.

Under Ask for Help:

- Identify your team—the people you will bring in to help you overcome this sticky place. Write their names down.

- Write down what you are willing to stop trying to control, surrendering instead to the Universe. It is an ask for help from the divine.

As an example, this is my compassionate plan for the story I shared at the beginning of this chapter:

Sticky Place: My eating and my weight

Action	Plan
Honor Yourself	I will keep track of my eating, my mood, and how they relate to each other. I will keep my cupboards clear of foods that trigger me to overeat. I will identify every time I hear me berating myself for decisions and actions that do not get me closer to what I want. I will practice the curiosity step. Whenever I sabotage myself, I will write in my journal what I've learned and next steps. I will share this struggle with three people close to me. I will continue with therapy sessions to discuss all that I learn and feel. I will stop using food to celebrate milestones in my life I will come up with ways to celebrate that help me stay on my path. Create a celebration chart of things I love and can choose from that do not include food.
Embrace Your Feelings	I will let myself grieve all the missed opportunities and happiness because of my weight. Will allow myself to cry or get angry in a safe space. I will start by celebrating every 7 days of tracking my food and my mood by choosing something from my celebration chart I will review this chart every month and challenge myself a little more in any of the areas mentioned in my plan
Ask for Help	PHYSICAL: Massages every 2 months to help me celebrate and connect with my body. Do TRE every week to start clearing trauma from the past. Dance workouts and yoga weekly. EMOTIONAL: Visit my therapist every month. Practice curiosity daily as I recognize things that take away my peace. ENERGETIC: Practice self-reiki as needed. I will surrender the number on the scale to the universe. My commitment will not be to a number but to a feeling. I will enjoy the feeling of pride that I am taking care of my body and the feeling of strength whenever my body accomplishes a new thing it couldn't do before.

Sí, Pero

- **"I can't stop berating myself!"** Chica, if this is the case, there may be some very ingrained voices in you from your past, maybe a strict mother or a rigid teacher. Do the curiosity step, and, if possible, connect with a professional who can help you. More important, recognize this is not your voice and that it's okay to let it go. In its place, practice speaking to yourself in a loving voice. You can do "mirror work," as created by Louise Hay and described in her book *Mirror Work: 21 Days to Heal Your Life*. Look deep into your own eyes in a mirror and say "I love you. I really, really love you." Every time you pass a mirror, say an affirmation or tell yourself "I love you."

- **"I am compassionate, but now I have so much compassion I can't get stuff done."** Go back to the difference between indulging and supporting. Playing the old story of "my life is so unfair" is indulging yourself, but taking action to change it is supportive. If you are indulging, you are not being compassionate, you are allowing yourself to be stuck. And that is not compassionate.

Chapter 7

Step 6:
CONTINUITY

Do Not Let It Get
This Bad Again

"Sandra, do not let it get this bad again."

Elizabeth, my therapist, looked me in the eyes as she handed me a letter in an envelope. It was our last session before my move to Europe with my husband. I was nervous but also filled with hope, and I assumed what she was handing me was a good luck letter. I looked at the envelope and then looked at Elizabeth with a questioning expression.

Elizabeth told me, "This is the letter you wrote for our first session, where you described your life."

I quickly responded, "But I threw that in the garbage."

Elizabeth told me, "I know. I retrieved it from the garbage can. I smoothed it and saved it all these years."

My eyes welled up with tears, and all I could say was a choked thank you. Elizabeth had just handed me a reminder of the girl I had been five years before, when I first walked through the doors of her office.

I said my good-bye and walked to my car. Once inside, surrounded by the darkness of the night, and with the dome light in my car as the only source of light, I read the letter.

I was now indeed a very different person from the person who had written this letter years before, and it hurt me to remember who I was back then. And I cried. I cried for the sad and hopeless girl who wrote that letter. I cried because I could feel her broken heart through every one of her sentences on the paper. I wanted nothing more than to hug her and tell her things would work out in the end. I cried in gratitude for the opportunity she created for me when she decided to take back the reins of her life. I cried for every time she read a new book, listened to new inspiration she received, or studied how to heal her broken heart. She is my hero.

Now I was ready to continue putting everything I had learned into practice in this new chapter of my life. I knew I had learned everything I needed to manifest the life I wanted and maintain the peace I had sought for so long and was now experiencing.

Through my head, however, ran the incessant questions: Can I make it on my own? Can I truly be free to live and create the life I want? And I heard Elizabeth's voice repeat, "Sandra, do not let it get this bad again." Little did I know that day, this was to become one of the mantras in my life.

Elizabeth had just reminded me with a simple phrase of the infinite power within me to create the life I wanted and of my responsibility to preserve the momentum I had created.

Let me back up a bit.

I'd been working with Elizabeth for five years when I was given the opportunity at work to take on an international assignment to become the R&D lead for one of our sites in Europe. This was all I had dreamed of! However, since this meant leaving my city, it also meant putting my sessions with Elizabeth on hold. I was so proud of everything I had accomplished during those years, and so grateful for everything Elizabeth had done for me.

In the years that followed that last session, I was tested in many ways at work and with health issues.

I knew how to create things in my life, I was even aware of curiosity and compassion, but soon I learned I didn't know yet how to "dance" with life. I kept trying to shove down my feelings to the darkest corners within myself whenever they showed up. I allowed myself to get so busy that I forgot to be present, and instead of becoming curious or compassionate, I would go from activity to activity unconsciously.

Life happens and it is rarely a smooth line. Everything can be going great until something happens that knocks the wind out of you. And although it does not seem like it, it's all perfect and part of the plan, getting you exactly to where you need to be.

Over the years that followed my move, challenging and unexpected days showed up in my life that triggered old belief systems such as *I am not good enough* and *I don't deserve*, and I lost some of the ground I had gained. I started once again feeling like life was happening *to* me, instead of *for* me. I became involved in the drama and hopelessness that comes with living a "life by accident." I walked through life as if on autopilot, paying no attention to my feelings.

When I finally felt the pain and suffering, I had drifted so far away from myself that I looked like a desperate version of me, frantically trying to keep my head above water as undesired things completely out of my control happened around me. At times it felt like I was drowning. I had lost the connection with myself. I cried often and found myself hopeless, with no idea of how to regain my joy. I had forgotten myself.

During those hard times, I would try to align my energy only to find that I was deep in desperation. I would try to become curious and have compassion, only to once again get caught up in the stories of the drama I was living. I felt like I couldn't get it together again.

And then, in a moment of inspiration from the Universe, Elizabeth's words came to me: "Sandra, do not let it get this bad again." I realized I had let it get bad again. Her words helped me pause, and although it took me a while to remember my power, I started to slowly reconnect with the light inside of me.

I once again became clear on where I was and where I wanted to go. Slowly I got in sync with myself and my desires. I started drafting tentative plans while surrendering my outcome to the Universe. I ruthlessly removed things and people from my life that did not contribute to the person I wanted to become or to the energy level I wanted to maintain. I became very picky about who I shared my space with and the situations I accepted. As I started once again connecting with my true self and my power, I started to see my life turn around.

It was as if I was a sailor who had completely let go of my sails and let the storm drag me to places I didn't want to go. As I remembered Elizabeth's words, I once again took control of my sails, and using the clarity of where I wanted to go, I navigated as needed. Although the wind blew in different directions, I just kept adjusting my sails to arrive at my desired destination.

I realized I knew how to create the life I wanted, but I had just gotten confused and allowed emotions to take over once again. I had allowed myself to disconnect from my true self. It was during this time that I learned that I don't have control over what happens in my life, but I *always* have control over how I respond to it. That's where intention happens, in how I respond to life. And for me to respond, I need to be connected with myself—not with other people's expectations of me, or with my sticky place, but with my authentic self.

I learned to ride the waves. I once again started connecting to my inner wisdom by becoming present with myself and my feelings, by becoming curious about things that took away my peace and compassionately allowing healing to happen around those areas. I deployed a loving approach to my life, putting my foot down and enacting boundaries that allowed me once again to create a safe space around me and inside of me. I gathered a team to support me through this, including fabulous mentors and my supportive family, starting with my husband and our new baby. I realized that this is a forever practice, and that my superpower was not going to be perfection, but resilience.

Being resilient is the art of recovering quickly from difficulties. That is now my superpower: my ability to come back to center again and again, regardless of what happens around me. I understand that things will happen. It's an inevitable part of life, and life can move forward only when I desire something different. Without this gap between where I am and where I want to be, life wouldn't be as exciting.

When I'm in the gap, the call is for me to be present. It's for me to know when something is taking away my peace and respond so I can get back to me quickly. I must respond before allowing whatever happens to take on a life of its own and make me feel groundless, desperate, and hopeless once again.

I knew the way, and I just needed to connect to myself to find it. In retrospect, I know now that one of the things that got me so confused during that time was that I once again became numb to my feelings.

By dealing with the day-to-day, I forgot to check in with myself and how I was feeling. I ignored all the signs. Before therapy, I had become so good at ignoring my feelings, the moment I was away from Elizabeth, I went back to old patterns. I stopped listening to myself. But our spirit always has a way to get our attention. At its worst, it does so with disease or constant suffering, but long before that, our spirit calls out our name in ways we can learn to identify. But for us to listen to its whispers, we need to be relentless witnesses of our life.

Witnessing Our Lives

We all need someone to witness our lives.

From a young age, we look up to our parents for their approval, later expanding that circle to tías y tíos (aunts and uncles), primos (cousins), vecinos (neighbors), etc. As we grow, we look for classmates, co-workers, and the cute boy we want to notice us to witness our life.

When someone becomes our witness, we feel like we matter, like we exist. We feel like we are worth it.

Because of this belief, soon we may find ourselves ignoring our own feelings and needs in order to keep people's attention on us. We may even learn certain tricks to keep their attention, like crying and making puppy faces so mamá comes and cuddles us, getting in trouble at school so papá spends time with us even if it involves attending a teacher-parent conference, or working day and night to get good grades so our parents brag about us to the tías.

We learn to confuse attention with love. We may have even learned that love and attention are conditional on us being a niña buena (good girl). Soon we learn that if we behave in ways that are not acceptable, we may get the ley del hielo (law of the ice) and be ignored until enough time had passed to remind us how fragile and conditional the love of others is. And as adults, we continue these patterns. Forsaking ourselves and our desires in the hope that we can make someone look at us, approve of us, or love us. We dance to their tune in hopes that they'll witness our life. This leads to feeling loneliness and overall dissatisfaction with life as we betray ourselves in our desire to be seen. We are driven by a fear of being left alone. And as is customary when we are driven by fear, nothing can fill that void.

But we keep trying, harder and harder, more and more, while ignoring ourselves. Our emotions are always talking to us, but over time we become so good at seeking people's validation that we forget to listen to our feelings.

We also become good at ignoring our feelings as a way to ser fuerte (be strong); after all, we were frequently told, "No llores o te doy una razón para llorar" ("Don't cry or I'll give you a reason to cry").

At times, we also ignore our feelings as a way to protect ourselves from pain, without understanding that pain multiplies and grows when ignored. After all, pain also wants to be witnessed. The result is that we become numb to ourselves and our lives.

Yet our feelings are always there, regardless of whether or not we pay attention to them. They are there to celebrate our highs, warn us when there is something bothering us, or implore us when there is the urgent need to grieve. They tell us when a relationship is not feeling right anymore, or when a job doesn't feel authentic to us any longer. They tell us when we are stuck in a past event that we wish had been different and is now causing us to feel depressed, or when we are anxious because we are scaring ourselves about an event that hasn't happened yet. We are anywhere but in the present, in our bodies.

Our feelings tell us when our heart has been broken. When feelings look to get our attention, we go back to our pattern of seeking someone external to us to make these feelings more tolerable by witnessing our pain and hoping they will fix it for us.

However, as we learned in Step 4: Curiosity, it is never about what happens to us, but about the thoughts we have about the situation. And no one can change those except ourselves. It is impossible to become curious about feelings when we are numb to them.

This step seeks to bring you back to yourself. To become your own witness. To do this, you need to reconnect with your feelings and make this connection a daily practice.

Continuity is an invitation to stay in constant contact with yourself, becoming aware of feelings that take away your peace—even the little ones, for they are the early warnings of what may become a landslide if you ignore them.

Once you identify an uncomfortable feeling happening, you can go back and become curious about it in an effort to heal or challenge your thoughts about it. You can recognize your triggers and confront them for your growth. You can take compassionate action to help you through a difficult time. You can align your energy back to the energy of well-being by going through your feelings with curiosity and compassion.

At the beginning, expect that this may take time and may require constant reminders to connect. Over time, however, you will be able to distinguish when a feeling is tugging at your sleeve to pay attention and witness it, just like an ignored child seeks their mami's attention and her gaze when they need someone to comfort them and make them feel safe.

Once you become a witness to your own life, you will start to lose this dependency on having someone else pay attention to it. Your inner self will feel listened to and pro-tected. It will feel seen, and by your compassionate actions you will make your inner self feel safe. In this space, once again you will be able to listen to the whispers of the Uni-verse as the voices in your head no longer feel the need to shout to be heard. The Universe will then talk to you about the inspired plans it has for you. But to get there, you need to be present and willing to get quiet and listen.

Once in this space, you can apply all the tools you have now learned. What brings you down in this journey is not being unsure of what to do, but not paying atten-tion to what is going on so you can address it as life is asking you to.

Continuity is also an invitation to witness your ups and downs, your joy and your pain—to be present as life happens and be there for yourself. To remember that it was never about the happy ending, but instead about the joyful life that you decide to bring about, moment by moment, breath by breath, by choosing to take the next best step that will get you closer to what you want—regardless of the circumstances you may be experiencing at the moment—with full honesty and in accordance with who you authentically are.

You go through life feeling lonely, longing for someone. You want someone to witness your life, to find a way to feel home. But as my friend Julia reminded me in one of our beautiful conversations, that someone that we long for is us. It was always us that we were missing.

Welcome home.

The Tell

Now, there will be times when witnessing may need to go beyond seeking to connect with your emotions, especially if you have a long history of ignoring your feelings. If that is the case, your spirit has a way to help. Your spirit has a tell.

Besides emotions, there is another kind of tell that your spirit will use to call your attention. It's known as a behavioral tell. I have already mentioned the emotional tell, where your spirit communicates to you that something needs your attention by the way you feel.

When you feel any of the manifestations of fear outlined in Chapter 5, that is a clear indication that you are not in sync with the Universe living in the present, and instead, you are letting a fear take over. However, if, like me, you have a master's degree in ignoring your feelings, there may not be an alarm system that will be loud enough to alert you, at least in the beginning. You might walk around saying, "Sé fuerte, mija" ("Be strong, my daughter"), plowing through and ignoring yourself. If that is the case, there is another way you can know you're letting fear win.

We all have behavioral tells. A behavioral tell is one or more behaviors that you do consistently when tension starts to build up inside you, sometimes even before you notice it yourself. They are physical things that you do obsessively as you are immersed in your stories and your feelings about the situation. They are meant to help you escape the uncomfortable feelings and keep you "safe" from pain in the moment. They also lead to the same outcome: refusal to accept reality and to take compassionate action to make it better. They are not planned or very noticeable to you; they are instead quite unconscious. Chances are you don't even catch yourself doing them. Until now.

Behavioral tells can be characterized as three kinds of behaviors:

1. **Numbing.** In this category are behaviors that you use to take your attention away from what is causing you stress or pain, in order to create a feeling of numbness around the uncomfortable thing. The end result is not thinking about what is bothering you, solving it, or even acknowledging it, but instead immediately neutralizing whatever uncomfortable feelings come up through mindless actions that can transport you to a more comfortable reality. They are like anesthesia for your emotional pain. Some examples of numbing actions can be Internet surfing, drinking, drugs, sex, binge eating, watching television, shopping, exercising excessively, traveling, focusing on other people's problems, etc.

2. **Soothing.** This is a behavior that allows you to "do something" while you are alone with your feelings and thoughts while providing some kind of relief, so that you can obsess in your head over the problem, massaging it but not necessarily solving it. Just like a baby with a chupón (pacifier), these actions take the edge off. The end result is you spending an endless amount of time just thinking about things without taking action, going around and around in a never-ending carousel that feels like a trance. This allows the constant song in your head to play on repeat. Examples might be biting your nails, playing with your hair, isolating yourself, telling everyone your woes, biting a pen, etc.

3. **Controlling.** This is a behavior you do to try to seek order in the chaos. This is about finding areas that you can make better, even if they are not at all related to the area that needs your attention. The end result is feeling like you are resolving something, even if it is not what needs resolution. It is a distraction strategy that provides relief by helping you feel like you have some kind of control over the uncontrollable. This could include picking fights with others over things that aren't important; completing chore lists incessantly that have nothing to do with the issue at hand; becoming inflexible about your kids' behavior and how they "should" behave; or tidying up and cleaning your place, your car, your desk, your files, your e-mails, etc.

My tells are overeating, tidying up obsessively (my home, the files in my computer, my e-mails, etc.), and biting my nails. When I start to repeat these behaviors consistently, I know there is something I am refusing to pay attention to.

Once you recognize a tell, it's a call to start paying very close attention to your feelings and the issues you are trying to numb, soothe, or control. As you experience your feelings, you can then apply the Curiosity and Compassion steps to understand what is behind them. As you integrate your feelings and lovingly tend to your wounds, the Universe whispers become easier to hear and your life starts aligning with the source of well-being.

¿Y Cómo?

Witnessing Your Life Exercise

The objective of this exercise is to start strengthening the connection between your mind and your heart by artificially reminding you to witness yourself.

In your phone, set an alarm for every three hours. For example, if you wake up at 7 A.M., you would set your alarm for 7 A.M., 10 A.M., 1 P.M., 4 P.M., 7 P.M., and 10 P.M. Write in the alarm "Witness!" or some catchy phrase so this shows up on your screen every time it buzzes.

When an alarm goes off, stop what you are doing, close your eyes, breathe, and quickly connect with your heart and ask yourself, *What am I feeling?* Sometimes, it could be boredom or contentment. Other times, it could be anxiety or sadness, or it might be joy and excitement. If any of those feelings are taking away your peace, become curious about them as described in the Curiosity step.

As you do this, you may notice yourself stopping and connecting with your inner self even when the alarm is not on. That is the practice of continuity.

Your Tells Exercise

The objective of this exercise is to identify the behavioral tells your spirit uses to get your attention when fear starts to rise.

Start by finding a time when you will not be interrupted and a place where you can be by yourself. Decide at the beginning of this exercise that you will be honest—brutally honest.

Remember three recent stressful situations that occurred in your life. Identify the feelings that you experienced about the situation, as well as the physical and behavioral cues you observed along with them. Use the chart below to record them. You can download the template for this exercise at www.sandrahinojosaludwig.com/chicawhynot.

Situation	Feeling	Tell Observed (numbing, soothing, controlling)
(1)		
(2)		
(3)		

Some questions that may help are:

- What are actions that you do consistently when feeling angry, sad, or anxious?
- How do you show nervousness or hopelessness?
- How do you communicate uneasiness to others?

Here is an example of a completed chart:

Situation	Feeling	Tell Observed (numbing, soothing, controlling)
(1) The doctor's office had me make a follow-up appointment to discuss my test results.	(1) Anxiety that I may have something serious. Impatience to find out why I'm called into the office. Sick to my stomach that my worst nightmares may become true.	(1) I watched TV all afternoon, ignoring everyone around me.
(2) My boss told me the report I prepared was not good enough. He said he was surprised and disappointed by my lack of attention to detail.	(2) Hurt and embarrassed. Feel scolded, like a child reprimanded by a parent. Blaming others for distracting me from my work.	(2) I picked fights with at least 3 different people that day.
(3) My car is on its last leg. I need to buy a new one, but my credit score is not as good as it needs to be.	(3) Stressed and worried over the uncertainty. I feel hopeless and unable to solve this.	(3) I bit my nails and fingertips raw. By the time I noticed I was biting down to the quick!

Sí, Pero

"I don't have any behavioral tells!" If you are older than preschool age, you have tells. You just haven't noticed them yet. Complete the tell exercise outlined above, and if you still can't figure out a tell, pay close attention whenever you catch yourself feeling anxious, sad, or angry, or having any feeling that is taking away your peace. If still it is hard to find one, ask some close friends about it. Questions you can ask them include:

- Have you noticed anything I consistently do when stressed?
- Is there anything specific I do when caught in thought?
- Is there a time when you find me irritable or moping around? What do I look like when I'm doing this?

A Love LETTER

El Camino por Caminar (The Path Yet to Be Walked)

Chica, estas lista. (You are ready.)

You now have all you need to step authentically into the world and intentionally create a life that loves you back.

You may still feel a bit nervous and hesitant; you may even be thinking, *Who am I to deserve all that I ever dreamed of?*

Chica, who are you not?

You are the perfect manifestation of the Universe put on this Earth to shine your light brightly so that the world may be better because of it. You are the descendant of powerful and beautiful women who stood tall and proud, regardless of their own brokenness. They gave you all they had, even if it never felt like enough. You come from the land where blood unites us but love keeps us together, where the bird sings and the sun reminds us of what a hug feels like.

You are one of the powerful Latinas in this world, bringing a song and a dance, full of love and promise. Your story has brought you here, and now it's your turn to claim all you deserve. The Universe has been waiting for you to be ready.

Well, you are ready now, mi amor.

The knowledge you have now about how the Universe works cannot be ignored any longer. Take all that you have learned about yourself and the Universe, and love yourself through the process of becoming a magnificent creator.

You are the writer of your own story. You get to pick the next chapter, and the one after that, and the one after that. And your book is a story of love and redemption, of peace and joy. You no longer give anyone else the power to write it for you. Show the world all that you can create, live, and love.

Know that as you consciously and intentionally create, your past may jump at you, poke you in the ribs, tell you stories, and make you wonder whether you can do this. It will try to make you fearful about the future and make you doubt your abilities. After all, you carry with you stories of hurt that go back for generations.

Chica, the past is only trying to remind you of all you have learned and all that is left to heal. Be grateful for those memories that every now and then will jump out at you and tell you stories that make you feel like you are not worth it. Mija, you are!

As those stories show up, like ghosts from the past, listen to them. Patiently and lovingly become curious about them. Then, with never-ending compassion, allow yourself to stay with the pain, and embrace it lovingly. The pain was always meant to become part of you, to become your guide and teacher. Do not run away from it. Simply sit with it, and love yourself compassionately through the process of healing it. By doing this, you are healing the world, starting by healing all the women who will come after you, wrapped in tamal leaves and with the sweet taste of cocoa on their lips.

As you repeat this cycle of healing, over and over, a peace you never knew was possible will set in. You will find yourself shedding tears, but this time those tears will be of happiness and joy. You will experience what full alignment with the Universe feels like. It feels like infinite possibilities, like a warm embrace, like sunrise. It feels like coming home.

Estás de nuevo en tu casa. (You are once again home.)

All of those times that you felt you needed to control, or those times you couldn't trust, will now become but a memory of the past. Complete faith in the Universe and its well-being will take its place.

You will now move easily, almost effortlessly, through the world. Life's uncertainties will no longer cause you anxiety; instead, they will make you hopeful about the future potential. Not having a full vision for your life will no longer feel like fear, it will feel like possibilities and like destiny manifesting.

Things may happen—in fact, I can assure you things *will* happen. But they won't terrify you anymore, because you now know you have all it takes to deal with those things that will show up. Your story is no longer about perfection, but about resilience. It is not about control, but about surrender.

You will now understand that the goals you have are no longer the end result, but the path you take to get there. Life becomes about the journey, about being present, about loving yourself into a life that will inevitably love you back.

Amiga, your heart is out of its cage and can now love in its full size, knowing that the hurt from yesterday can no longer touch it, and that the hurt from tomorrow will only teach you how to love yourself even more.

Enjoy this new season in your life—it will only keep getting better.

Eres libre. (You're free.)

ACKNOWLEDGMENTS

I am so grateful for all the amazing people who helped me bring this book and its message to life. Thank you to the whole team at Hay House for your support and mentoring through the process of launching my first book.

To Jeremey, my husband and best friend, and to Hobey, my son and biggest teacher, I love you. Thank you for being my partners in adventure.

Mi amor y cariño a las mujeres que siempre me han apoyado, en las buenas y en las malas, en las lágrimas y en las pachangas: a mi mamá, Rosaura Verdín; a mis hermanas, Laura Karina y Rosaura; y a mis amigas Marta Perales, Giulia Carcione, Joanna Kapusta y Karen Sterling.

My infinite gratitude to Debbie Weiler, for helping me reconnect with the fire inside me; to Brette Sember, for your guidance on how to put it in writing; and to Alex Ferreira, for your help expressing it as art.

Thank you to the best mentors a chica could ask for: Kelly Notaras, Rebecca Campbell, Anne Bérubé, Paul MacInnis, Chaz Thorne, Christel Leblanc, Christine Gutiérrez, Juliet Diaz, Harry Lopez, and Ana Sheila Victorino.

And to every Latina that has allowed me to be part of their journey toward intentionally manifesting a life that loves them back: Gracias, chicas, por su amor, confianza e inspiración. Your light makes my life brighter. Las quiero mucho.

ABOUT THE AUTHOR

Sandra Hinojosa Ludwig is a certified life coach from the Transformational Arts College in Toronto, Canada. Through her Facebook and Instagram communities, as well as her nonprofit coaching program and her Chica Catalyst, she helps Latinas intentionally manifest a life that loves them back. Through individual and group coaching, Sandra has connected with women from all over the Americas, including the United States, Canada, Argentina, Chile, Colombia, Mexico, and Peru.

After leaving her childhood home of Monterrey, Mexico, Sandra poured herself into a successful corporate career that took her to Germany, the United States, the United Kingdom, and ultimately to Canada, where she now resides. Tired from trying to unsuccessfully chase happiness, she turned to therapy and spirituality for help, eventually becoming a certified life coach, Reiki practitioner, and a certified angel card reader. For more on Sandra's work, visit www.sandrahinojosaludwig.com.

We hope you enjoyed this Hay House book. If you'd like to receive our online catalog featuring additional information on Hay House books and products, or if you'd like to find out more about the Hay Foundation, please contact:

Hay House, Inc., P.O. Box 5100, Carlsbad, CA 92018-5100
(760) 431-7695 or (800) 654-5126
(760) 431-6948 (fax) or (800) 650-5115 (fax)
www.hayhouse.com® • www.hayfoundation.org

———

Published in Australia by: Hay House Australia Pty. Ltd.,
18/36 Ralph St., Alexandria NSW 2015
Phone: 612-9669-4299 • *Fax:* 612-9669-4144
www.hayhouse.com.au

Published in the United Kingdom by: Hay House UK, Ltd.,
The Sixth Floor, Watson House, 54 Baker Street, London W1U 7BU
Phone: +44 (0)20 3927 7290 • *Fax:* +44 (0)20 3927 7291
www.hayhouse.co.uk

Published in India by: Hay House Publishers India,
Muskaan Complex, Plot No. 3, B-2, Vasant Kunj, New Delhi 110 070
Phone: 91-11-4176-1620 • *Fax:* 91-11-4176-1630
www.hayhouse.co.in

———

Access New Knowledge.
Anytime. Anywhere.

Learn and evolve at your own pace
with the world's leading experts.

www.hayhouseU.com

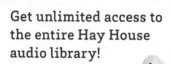